24/7 Living
Hard Truths from James

Terry W. Pollard

In loving memory of
my role model father, pastor-shepherd, spiritual mentor,
and prince of preachers
who was faithful in life and in death.
Rev. Dr. Raymond E Pollard, Jr.
Thanks for helping shape who I am as a pastor and leader.
I can't wait to see you when we all get home to heaven.

Acknowledgements

No person becomes who they are alone. No book is written by the author alone. I claim little originality. I am the beneficiary of so many on my faith journey.

Special thanks to Mark Avery, Lyle Parker, Ruby Mays-Rice, and so many other life-long friends for their willingness to indulge in some review reading before this book was published and everyone at Steuben Press for their fine expertise in helping make my dream possible.

Few of the ideas in this book are original to the author; most have been borrowed from better minds and hearts which belong to the tens and tens of books I have read on James and all the notes I've made from their writings in sermons and teaching notes I have used to share with my congregations around the country. I claim nothing new at all. I only know some of my sources.

Thanks to Lavonne Pollard-Maddox, who exemplifies all that is good and right and lovely about the word "Mom." I love you, Mom. You are the charter member of my "fan club!"

Thanks also to the rest of my family, especially my three loving children and their spouses, Chad and Karey, Lance and Mandi, and Leandra and Matt, as well as my blended family children, Bradley and Elissa, Danny and Courtney, and all their beautiful and fun-filled children whom I gladly claim as my precious grandchildren, and my many friends who are too numerous to mention without making this sound self-indulgent and sappy. The privilege of your love and friendship enriches my soul. I am forever blessed because of you.

Thanks to all my parishioners and students in more than 38 years of pastoral, teaching and para-church ministry, both at home and overseas, who have listened to my preaching and teaching and read my writings and helped me dig a little deeper. I am a better person in my faith journey because of you.

Last, but in no way least, thanks to my dear wife and best friend for life, Diana, who keeps the whimsy alive and who single-handedly proves the existence of beauty, loyalty, passion, and wisdom. I love you.

PREFACE

This book in your hands is like a "crash course" about suffering and living the Christian life. Like in the days of Job in the Old Testament, there are still those who consider suffering and trials to be the result of disobedience. Terry Pollard offers hope to all stating that "the junk of life" is not the ending, but can be the beginning of realization that God will bring beauty from ashes and puzzling brokenness into a collage of completeness. The ringing message of this book is hope rather than despair in the trials, losses, set-backs and confusion of life. Encouragement is at the heart of this author's writing. He deeply cares and loves those under his watch.

As you read this book, you will sense the call to hope when the storms of life rage, and circumstances of life beat against our minds, souls and body. If there ever were a day when this message is needed, it certainly is in this day.

Terry Pollard wants to get our attention in this message so that our faith may grow and not diminish and so that our response to life will deepen us in a life of growing faith in God. How we respond to the mysterious difficulties of life will make us a better person or will break us into despair and hopelessness.

This is the underlying concern of the author of the Book of James and Terry Pollard who has experienced "the junk of life" but who, by the marvelous grace of God, has permitted those things to make him a better person, a better leader, a more caring and effective pastor.

His message of hope uses imagery such as "the race of life", "God's winner's circle", and "the crown of life". What a message in stormy times!

As you carefully read this book, you will feel the love that comes through the writer's pen encouraging us to keep *the big picture of life* which includes confidence in God's grace to transform, cleanse, and liberate us from the stuff that life throws at us and we can live life 24/7 with courage.

Join me and the writer in discovering that God offers hope for all who believe and submit to Him.

Lyle G. Parker
Retired Elder, Church of the Nazarene
Kansas City, Kansas

FOREWORD

Terry sang in a public relations quartet representing Kansas City College and Bible School, now Kansas Christian College. I was in my late teens when that quartet sang at my local church in Ann Arbor, Michigan. Within a year, I enrolled at KCCBS and thus began a friendship that has lasted for many years. Terry and I shared many classes together as both of us sensed God's call in our lives. Theology, Greek, various Bible classes and ministry classes helped to form both of us into the men we have become today.

Our ministries have paralleled in many ways. We have both spent time in pastoral ministry and both happily state that pastoring churches is our passion. Pastor Terry Pollard was called out of pastoral ministry for a few years to serve as Editor of Publications at Herald and Banner Press in Overland Park, Kansas. Several years later, I followed him in that position. For a few years Terry served as Youth Editor while I was his "boss" as Editor of Publications.

Terry and I shared ministry together. We have served on General Church committees together and Terry preached a revival in one of the churches I pastored early in my ministry.

Once, during a very dark time in Terry's life, I was privileged to be a special friend and confidant to him. Our relationship deepened. Terry and I talked together, prayed together, counseled and sought answers from God's Word together. Terry remains my friend.

While many others rightly call Terry their friend, Terry is more. Anyone who has sat under his ministry also recognizes him as a scholar. That is not new with Terry. The scholarship that distinguished him in his college days has accompanied him throughout his ministry. Too often, scholarship is detached from life, but not so with my friend. Terry's scholarship has challenged himself and his people to put the Bible into practice in life. This book, based on the very practical New Testament Epistle written by James, is intensely practical.

One character trait of true scholarship is the ability to be understood. Without forfeiting scholarship and without talking down to his readers, Terry has written a practical, readable book that serious Christians, educated and uneducated, will find useful and understandable.

Balance is an important concept in Christian living. Most of the Christian world believes in salvation by grace. Yet we often struggle to figure out how to get our outward works to match the inward effects of grace. Grace makes changes. James talked about that. "Show me your faith without your works and I'll show you my faith by my works." Any time I'm hungry, I'd rather be cared for by someone who would bless me with food than someone who merely blessed me with words.

James understood that Christianity is practical. Terry understands that, too. This book will challenge you to put your faith into practice. In a society where perhaps 80 percent of church members have little involvement outside the Sunday morning worship service, Terry reminds us that living the Christian life is a 24/7/365 proposition. I gladly commend this book to you.

Mark Avery, Pastor
Church of God (Holiness), Mexico, Missouri

AUTHOR'S PREFACE

Dear Reader, I like things that work. When something is broken, I want it fixed soon. I do not like to wait. If it is broken, I can't use it and it's not worth much to me or anyone.

That is why I have come to love the little New Testament Letter of James. Across my more than 38 years of pastoral and teaching ministry, I have undoubtedly read this book more than any other book in the Bible. I think I almost have it memorized. It is my go-to book when I want practical and livable advice about what it means to follow Christ.

For a long time, it has been my desire to take the compilation of my many preaching and teaching notes on James and wrap them all into a short book. It was no easy task. But here it is and I am glad to share some of what I have learned from this little "gospel of common sense" in the New Testament, as I like to call it. The reason I share this is because I have a simple, basic belief that if we are going to claim to be followers of Jesus Christ, then that claim needs to work in our lives every day. What we proclaim we must live – loud and clear. If, as followers of The Way, our walk and talk are broken then it needs to be fixed. And if it doesn't work for us, it won't work for anyone else, either. That's what this book you hold in your hand is all about. We must walk the talk.

My goal in sharing my insights with you is to take some pretty hard truths in the Book of James and put them into some plain language so we can know that what was written by James is just as contemporary for us in the 21st century as it was in the 1st century. It is truth for our times. So, I am prayerful that it helps you as it has helped me.

Warmly, Terry W. Pollard

CONTENTS

1

A MESSAGE THAT STICKS

"You must be doers of the word and not only hearers who mislead themselves" (James 1:22).

I well remember the words of my preacher father, Raymond, now deceased, who was also a pastor and a powerful communicator in preaching for over 25 years. His once-upon-a-time pithy expression about the teachings of the Book of James, which was a favorite of his as it is mine, still remains with me. He said, in short, that James is teaching us, "I don't care how high you jump, just be sure you walk straight when you come down." How true it is.

I think my preacher father described well the New Testament Book of James. This book is about as straight-forward book as you will find in the New Testament. It is one of the most practical, hard-hitting books of the Bible. It has been referred to as "the gospel of common sense." If you want practical, this book is for you.

The Book of James is one of seven letters in the New Testament that is identified as the "general" or "catholic" Epistles (catholic meaning "universal"). Unlike the letters of the apostle Paul, the Book of James is a more general letter written to the Church at large, rather than a specific congregation facing a particular set of circumstances.

In a historical context, we know that James, the writer, was sharing a letter in the form of a pastoral exhortation to Jewish Christians in the first century of the Christian church.

These Jewish Christians were scattered throughout Palestine and Syria. So, James begins his book by addressing his audience as "the twelve tribes who are scattered outside the land of Israel" (James 1:1). In a literal historical sense, he is writing to ethnic Jews; in this case, Jews who had come to faith in Christ and who had been dispersed from Jerusalem by persecution.

However, we also know that the word of God is timeless. Those Jews who were scattered can also be viewed in a figurative sense. In this way, James also wrote to believers today, who are scattered among the nations. It refers to all the people of God under the new covenant, both Jewish and Gentile Christians, who together are the spiritual descendants of Abraham (see Romans 4:16; 9:6-8; Galatians 3:16; 6:16). Although separated by nearly twenty centuries, our needs in the 21st century are very much the same and the message of James still needs to be heard and applied in our decaying culture.

These scattered Jewish Christians in the Early Church spread their newly found faith ". . . to the end of the earth" (Acts 1:8), preaching the good news of Jesus wherever they went (Acts 8:4). The result? Many new converts were added to the Christian faith. These first believers faced a great deal of persecution and hardship because of their allegiance to Jesus Christ. This early contagion of the spread of the Good News (the gospel) of Jesus created a climate for follow-up, spiritual instruction, and encouragement to these early converts to Christianity. So it was that James, the assumed leader of the Jerusalem Christian community and a spiritual shepherd to the scattered flock, wrote to this large group of Jewish Christians who were living in faraway places, having scattered because of persecution for their Christian faith.

James was concerned that his Christian sisters and brothers would persevere in their Christian faith, in spite of trials, persecutions, suffering, temptations and pressures, as followers of Christ in a world that was hostile to the message of Christianity. James encouraged his readers in the trials and tribulations of life and challenged them to engage in right living. He was concerned with the consistency of genuine faith as evidenced by its results. Faith should be active and evident, not just a mere profession.

James' overall message is a compelling one that challenges Christians to live a life of true religion and heart holiness towards God and man.

James understood that there are two sides to the gospel; the *believing* side and the *behaving* side. James does not discount or diminish the *believing* side of the gospel. Rather, he chose to make his chief concern the *behaving* side. He is concerned with *conduct*, not *creed*. He is concerned with *behavior*, not just *belief*. For James, faith is not something merely *believed*; it is something we *do*. It is something we live out daily in active obedience to Christ as His follower.

For James, it is deeds that demonstrate an authentic faith. The way believers *behave* and *live* must correspond to the claims they make about their faith – what they believe. James attacks the contradictions between faith and living. Faith is primary in his letter – but only faith which is true, active, consistent, genuine and clearly evident.

The message of James is important for us to understand. One of our tendencies as followers of Christ is to be long on *doctrinal conformity*, but short on *ethical consistency*. Faith and experience in the Christian life are of great importance. But faith and experience are of little value to anyone unless these two intertwined elements lead to consistent Christian living.

James is a book of practical theology with little doctrinal teaching. For James, faith in Jesus Christ involves *doing*, not just *being*. It is not enough just to listen to the word; it is truly a message to obey. We cannot just say we are believers or followers of Christ; we must show it by the way in which we live. James gives his wise instruction in a distinctive "where-the-rubber-meets-the-road" kind of way. He is concerned about the nitty-gritty of life. He is concerned about twenty-four hours, seven days (24/7) a week kind of living. In short, we can call it 24/7 living.

Believers must demonstrate right actions for the right reasons. Our faith must be evident in the way we control our tongue and relate to others. Submitting to God means that we live out what we say we believe. Prejudice is to be rebuked. Loving one's neighbor affects the tongue. The rich must share with the poor. Caring for the oppressed and the poor is a result of obedience to a just and righteous God.

It should be noted there is a higher percentage of commands in James than in any other book of the Bible. At least sixty of the 108 verses in the Book of James are set forth in the form of a command. James' frequent use of commands tells us a whole lot about his passionate feelings around the issues he knew faced the Early Church and even us today.

For James, there is no wiggle room in the way in which we are to live in obedience to Christ and His commands. James' readers were facing very difficult times and surely were tempted to take the easy way out and be in friendship with the world (James 4:4) so as to avoid persecution or hardship. There is no easy road or easy living.

The imperatives that James outlines in this five chapter book are clear cut commands that compel followers of Jesus Christ to live a life of true religion and holiness towards God and others. His fiery, pithy, and precise words resemble those of the Old Testament prophets. He writes in no uncertain terms. James shares ethical commands that touch upon personal morality and issues of social justice. What he says to us as followers of Christ is as contemporary as the 21st century in which we live. The issues he confronts head-on read like the daily newspaper.

When all is said and done, the pagan and hedonistic culture around us is often little concerned with what we actually believe, though it is vitally important. However, the pagan world is tremendously concerned with the way in which we live our lives. It is not what followers of Christ say they believe; but how they live out what they say they believe. Talk is cheap. In a word, James reminds us that we need to walk our talk. We need to live out the life of Christ 24/7.

We are what we are because we believe what we believe. One of the big struggles that people have with those who *profess* the life of Christ is those who do not *live* the life of Christ. It may be that those who profess the life of Christ look like Christians (whatever Christians are imagined to look like), talk like Christians, sing like Christians, but simply do not *act* like Christians.

A.W. Tozer, in his book entitled *Root of the Righteous*, laments with powerful words the discrepancy between the *profession* and *practice* of the Christian faith. He writes, "There is an evil which I have seen under the sun . . . It is the glaring disparity between theology and practice among professing Christians.

"So wide is the gulf that separates theory from practice in the church that an inquiring stranger who chances upon both would scarcely dream that there was any relation between them. An intelligent observer of our human scene who heard the Sunday morning sermon and later watched the Sunday afternoon conduct of those who had heard it would conclude that he had been examining two distinct and contrary religions . . . It appears that too many Christians want to enjoy the thrill of feeling right but are not willing to endure the inconveniences of being right. So the divorce between theory and practice becomes permanent, in fact, though in word the union is declared to be eternal. Truth sits forsaken and grieves till her professed followers come home for a brief visit, but she sees them depart again when the bills come due."

Many Christians end up with lives divorced from truth because they think that simply agreeing with Scripture is the same as obeying it. James urges his readers to go beyond preparing to hear the word of God or receive the word of God. It must be acted upon. We must live what we have heard. Do not just hear the word; live the word!

This is why James 2:18 becomes the key verse around which the Book of James forms its teaching. "Someone might claim, 'You have faith and I have action.' But how can I see our faith apart from your actions? Instead, I'll show you my faith by putting it into practice in faithful action."

Faith and works are not separate or alternate expressions of Christianity. No one is able to say, "You do your deeds and I will have my faith. We'll just follow Christ in our own way." James' message is that faith and works (actions or deeds) cannot be separated without ceasing to be alive, without ceasing to be a vital, active, visible and lived-out faith.

In simple terms, we can say that faith in Christ in our lives will find its truest expression in the action it generates in our lives. Actions require faith to have meaning. Faith cannot be shown apart from actions. While it is true that faith is within us, it can only be seen when actions arising from a genuine faith are produced through us. It is easy to say, "I'm a Christian" or "I am a follower of Christ"; it can be more difficult to fully live it out every day. James agrees that one is saved by faith alone and not by works, but he emphasizes that genuine faith produces fruit. Something distinctive and different happens in the lives of those who choose to follow Jesus Christ.

William Barclay, in his book on *The Letters of James and Peter*, reminds us that vital and faith-filled Christian living, what he calls "a well-proportioned life", is not to be represented as an "either-or" choice for us. It is actually a "both-and" choice in life.

In a well-proportioned life - a faith-filled life - there must be thought and action. That is, as Barclay suggests, "a thinker is only half a person unless the thoughts are turned into deeds, and will scarcely even inspire others to action unless he or she comes down into the battle and shares the arena with them." In short, there must be faith and action in our lives.

We can see, then, that there is no room for a workless faith. A *workless* faith is a *worthless* faith. The message of James is that any faith that does not move believers to action is also a faith that is not worth having or talking about. If our actions are not expressions of a saving and vital faith rooted in the grace and love of Christ, then our actions are nothing but pointless and feeble efforts.

Faith and deeds are not opposites; they are inseparable. According to James, no one is moved to action without faith, and faith is not genuine if it does not move us to action. It is not about choosing faith over works or works over faith. In short, it is about faith and deeds being but opposite sides of our experience of God.

As we shall see in our study of the Book of James and its varied topics, it is good deeds *after* conversion that are evidence of faith and a right relationship with God.

True faith produces good works. This is the heart and soul – the part and parcel – of the message of the Book of James.

I am quite fond of Coca-Cola®. In fact, I collect Coca-Cola® memorabilia as a fun hobby. My church office is full of all kinds of tokens that remind me I am surrounded by a sea of red and white. In fact, I have so much memorabilia I can't display it all! The Coca-Cola® company motto, branded clearly on all their products, is that their drink is the "Real Thing." Some will argue that it is not, especially if they like Pepsi or some other delicious, thirst-quenching drink. But the fact is when you see the Coca-Cola® brand name, you will be thinking about the "Real Thing."

James clear message is for followers of Christ not only to *possess the real thing* but also to *live the real thing.* James is all about the "Real Thing." The problems faced by James and the early Christians in the first century are just as prevalent today. Churches are filled with Christians who claim to be followers of Christ. Regretfully, however, too many are living a self-styled form of Christianity. Many of these professed followers of Jesus have hollow claims because they have a hollow faith. The fact is, too many seek to live a faith that belies their profession of faith because of actions and attitudes that are not Christ-like or Spirit-filled or by what they fail to do. There are, as we know, many different religions and, in fact, people who claim to be the "real thing." They offer religion without a relationship, a crown without a cross, salvation without a Savior, or peace without the Prince of Peace. They offer a Jesus that is not the same Jesus of the Bible. They offer a love that is not really God's kind of love.

Then there are others who choose to use Christ, Christianity, and the Church for personal gain (politicians who want votes, salespeople who want contacts, merchants who want customers, and yes, even preachers who want money) and they offer comfort without commitment. It has simply become a Christianity of convenient living. Indeed, a faith of some kind is offered, but it is not the real faith. It is not the "Real Thing."

Consider also that according to current polling data, most North Americans say they are Christians. But the reality is that this same data reveals most Westerners are amazingly biblically illiterate, not even able to name five of the Ten Commandments or the first four Gospels of the New Testament. And when we take a look at all the social needs of the 21st century – things like human sex trafficking, exploitation of women and children, poverty, homelessness, teenage pregnancy, racism, child abuse, substance abuse, divorce, single moms, the opioid crisis and so many other societal vices and woes – it makes one wonder and it is fair to ask, "If there are so many Christians, why do these problems still exist? What difference for Christ are all these Christians making, anyway? Where is the sustained impact on our culture?"

James' clarion call and concern is one of authentic Christian living. That is, it means that we practice a religion of wholehearted and undivided devotion to God rather than attempting to find a middle way between God and the world (James 4:4-8). That is why we need to listen again to the teaching from the Book of James. Much of the content of James represents an effort to call individuals and the Church back to full commitment to God and concern for one another. The call and message of James is to make a difference in this world with a genuine, saving faith that works. The call is to live out an authentic faith every day, every week, every month, and every year. It is a 24/7/365 kind of faith.

The teaching of James is relevant for all believers today. As James encouraged his readers in the trials and tribulations of life and challenged them to engage in right living in a morally bankrupt, truth-twisted and spiritually dark world, so also are we encouraged to do the same.

We cannot escape its message and profound implications for living today. This message cannot be pushed off as something followers of Christ need not hear, but only something for non-believers in a secular, pagan world.

This letter has lasting value and consequence to the Christian confronted by an increasingly secular world. The simple theme and clear mandate of James is that following Jesus Christ ought to make a difference in a believer's life. That mandate is truly as relevant today as it was when James wrote to his original readers. The application of the message in the Book of James is clear: the Church of Jesus Christ must consistently, wholeheartedly, unreservedly, courageously, boldly, unashamedly, unapologetically and continuously invite people to genuine faith in the Lord Jesus Christ. It should be and is a genuine faith that results in changed lives. To do less than this is to fail the gospel.

It is time for individual Christians who claim the name of Jesus Christ to evaluate their level of obedience to their Master, the Lord Jesus Christ, and live out what it means to be a "slave of God and of the Lord Jesus Christ" (James 1:1). It is time for Christians to recommit to doing the good works that result from a changed life of saving faith in Jesus Christ.

The apostle Paul, another New Testament writer, expressed a clarion call to us as followers of The Way. "Since we belong to the day, let's stay sober, wearing faithfulness and love as a piece of armor that protects our body and the hope of salvation as a helmet" (1 Thessalonians 5:8).

In a practical kind of way, the Book of James will help us understand how to do just that – think clearly (sober), be protected by faithfulness and love, and live out the confident hope of our salvation, grounded in the grace and mercy of Jesus Christ.

In order to live this authentic faith that James writes about, we need to live according to a comprehensively biblical world-view, with a right understanding of trials, suffering and temptation (James 1:2-11; 5:7-11), a right understanding of right conduct in contrast to mere doctrinal agreement (James 1:19-27; 2:14-26), a right understanding of appropriate speech (James 3:1-12); a right understanding of true wisdom (James 3:13-18); a right understanding of humility and pride (James 4:1-17), and a right understanding of poverty and wealth (James 2:1-13; 5:1-6).

From the central message that James shares about moving beyond mere words into action – living out our faith - to the main topics he unpacks for us that are as relevant in 21st century Christianity as they were in 1st century living, we can discover what practical Christianity is really all about. We can take a look at how each one is amplified throughout the Book of James – in just 108 verses. And we can consider the historical context of each topic, its meaning for first-century believers and the practical implication and application for us today.

The Book of James is our practical handbook for Christian living in a hostile and ungodly world. Each one of us should receive its teachings with meekness so that it may work in our lives to the salvation of our souls. It is high time to live the life 24/7!

Words to Live by from the Church Fathers

OECUMENIUS: *More than any worldly dignity, the Lord's apostles gloried in the fact that they were slaves of Christ. That is how they wanted to be known in their preaching, in their writing and in their teaching.*

DIDYMUS THE BLIND: *Those who seek worldly glory display the qualifications which they think they have in their correspondence. But the apostles boast, at the beginning of their letters, that they are slaves of God and Christ.*

HILARY OF ARLES: *James refers to himself as a servant, but we must remember that there are two kinds of servitude, voluntary and involuntary. The involuntary servant is a slave who fears punishment, and therefore his service does not spring from love. But the voluntary servant is really no different from a son.*

2

JOY IN THE JUNK OF LIFE
James 1:2-8, 12

"My brothers and sisters, think of the various tests you encounter as occasions for joy." (James 1:2)

On the cereal box of life, we are not told what to expect. No one tells us how good the highs can be and how bad the lows can get. I wish I could tell you that you will never have trouble in life. I wish I could tell you that living the Christian life is a very easy thing. But I can't do that. The reason is simple. Neither of these things is true.

There is a sign hanging on the bulletin board in a hospital where I visit parishioners frequently. It reads: "Be kind. For everyone you meet is fighting a battle."

When I was younger, I did not appreciate that sentiment like I do now. The older I get the more I realize that it is true. Everyone you meet is fighting a battle of one kind or another.

And it is certainly true of followers of Jesus Christ. It may be dealing with the loss of a loved one in death, taking care of aging parents, problems with our children or grandchildren, facing temptations of one kind or another, a debilitating illness or deadly disease, or financial problems. All of us have a commonality in that we face perplexing troubles.

We know first-hand that God indeed does call us to suffer – some of us much more than others. And all of us who place our trust in Jesus know full well that the Christian life often includes difficult trials designed to test our faith. Suffering, trials, temptations, and the testing of our faith, are all realities of the Christian life. All of these difficult issues are raised in the opening chapter of the Book of James, a letter written to persecuted Christians living during the most trying of times.

We all come to understand in some way that God uses difficult times to bring about the completeness of our faith. James tells us to "think of the various tests you encounter as occasions for joy. After all, you know that the testing of your faith produces endurance. Let this endurance complete its work so that you may be fully mature, complete, and lacking in nothing" (James 1:2-4).

Whenever trouble comes your way, let it be an opportunity for joy. I know how trite it can sound when someone quotes James and tells the sufferer to think of suffering or hardship as an occasion for joy. But James is not asking us to ignore our circumstances, to just suck it up, and be joyful, regardless. James is telling us that God allows trials to come for a reason. Trials make us steadfast. They allow us to strengthen our faith.

It is all about perspective. This is not joyful anticipation *for* trials. Rather, it is joy *during* trials. While we are told to be joyful in suffering, we also need to know that when we go through trials there is a purpose. Our faith is being tested. A faith tested is a faith that becomes steadfast, a faith that endures in difficult times, and a faith that becomes much stronger than it was before the trial.

Properly understood, trials represent the possibility of growth. This is not to suggest that following Christ is an easy way to go. It is quite the contrary. We all find ourselves involved in varied colored trials and hardships in life. The stark reality for all of us is that adversity in life takes on many forms. Troubles are what I call *"the junk of life."* And we all have troubles. We all have junk in our life. The trail of life is marked with junk. Trials come to us as part of our common humanity.

From where do the trials come? They can be troubles that happen from without or temptations from within. They can come when we are least prepared or when we think they could never come. It can be loneliness, grief, suffering, illness, debilitating or deadly disease, hardship, rejection, frustration, homesickness, social isolation, language barriers, or culture shock. And the trials faced can come from many different sources – friends, family, opponents, doubts, fears, adversity, or from our own choices we make in life. While we are free to choose, we are never free to choose the consequences.

We are called to be joyful - not *if* we face trials but *whenever* we face trials. When we encounter a trial, we really do not have the option to take it or leave it. It is an unwanted and unwelcome experience in our life. It is an unavoidable difficulty of life. We cannot get around it, no matter what.

There is no need to pretend to be happy when we face pain or trouble in life. Rejoicing goes beyond happiness. Happiness centers on what happens to us. If something good happens, like getting a pay raise, we are happy. If something bad happens, like losing our job, we are unhappy. Happiness depends on earthly circumstances and how well things are going here in life for us. Happiness is *event-oriented*. Joy is *God-oriented*.

Why is that? Because joy centers on God and His presence in our experiences of life. It is a contentment that comes from realizing that nothing can "separate us from God's love in Christ Jesus our Lord" (Romans 8:38).

Joy has to do with a perspective in life that comes from the inside out. This happens because of what trials can produce in our lives. We turn our hardships into times of learning. Tough times serve to teach us perseverance.

The tough times we experience in life are directed towards an end. The end is that anyone who is tested should emerge stronger and purer from the experience. Trouble does not come for trouble's sake; it is not an end in itself. We are not to thrash about in hopeless and despairing frustration as troubles come. When you are having trouble, do not start crying as if something strange or unusual has happened to you. You are to *rejoice* and count it all joy that God is testing you in this way. And we know that is not easy at all.

Saying that we are to rejoice is like putting together a puzzle with a missing piece in our life. Whatever trials we may be experiencing do not come about because God is retributively punishing us. Rather, trials come because God is allowing our faith to be tested so that our faith becomes stronger. It is so that we become steadfast and more resolute. So, when we accept trials in life as a means of testing and allow God to make us complete, He brings His work in us to its more perfect fruition.

Trials are like a refining fire. They are the means by which our faith is made strong, steadfast, built-up, and robust.

Suffering of any kind is horrible. No one wants to suffer. No one likes to suffer. No one chooses suffering just to suffer. But suffering does have a purpose in God's economy – even if that purpose is known only to God. When we follow Christ, we can know that trials become an occasion for joy because we know that God is working out His mysterious purposes in us. That purpose involves bringing us to maturity, to completeness.

The call to rejoice is a strange response to the difficulties of life. I do not like to be tested. I would rather that everything went very smoothly. I would rather that no one got in my way. I would rather that no one cross me. I would rather that no one cut in front of me in life. But it does not happen that way. Life is not that way. Life is filled with many disappointments.

There are always people around you who are going crosscurrent to you. There will always be people who will be irritants to you. There will always be an irritating situation.

I cannot rule and order my life, as I would have it. Neither can you. If I did, I would become spoiled, rotten and pompous. I would want everybody to bow. I would want everybody to yield. I would want everybody to submit. But it does not happen that way. And so for our growth, for our development, the trials of life are a necessary ingredient.

This is not to say that our trials should produce no other reaction but joy. Trying to deny our grief and sadness in loss or pretending that suffering is not painful is ultimately futile and that is not what is called for here. Nor does God condemn us as less than spiritual when we experience normal human emotions. Instead, what it does mean is that our joy in the midst of trials should be genuine and sincere. When these uninvited visitors arrive, we should choose to regard them as reasons for a higher purpose. When encountered, trials are to be endured and worked through. For the believer, this is a necessary process for maturing in the faith. We are able to do this because of the certainty that our difficulties, setbacks, and struggles are producing a result that is worth the cost in tears and sorrow. These things help us see life through a different lens.

How is it that trials and joy coexist? We cannot really know the depth of our character until we see how we react under pressure. It is easy to be kind to others when everything is going well, but can we still be kind when others are treating us unfairly? I am reminded of the story of the little girl who knelt beside her bed at the end of the day to pray. Her prayer was simple: "Lord, make all the *bad* people *good* and all the *good* people *kind*."

God wants to make us mature and complete, not to keep us from all pain. Instead of complaining about our struggles, we should see them as opportunities for growth. Our response should be gratitude to God for promising to be with us in rough times. Ask God to help you work through your problems or give you the strength to endure them. Then be patient. God will not leave you alone with your problems. He will stay close and help you grow.

God has a goal in mind — you can count on that. We are called to remember that when our faith is tested it produces endurance. It is all about the attitude of your heart toward your trouble. When trouble troubles you, what is your response? When the external pressures of testing are upon us and we are placed in the fires of adversity, tragedy or suffering, the attitude of faith should be that God has permitted it for a purpose – to prove our faith genuine. We can know that God is working something out in our lives.

This does not necessarily mean that we will *understand* what purpose God has in it. This is the test of *faith*. We walk by faith and not by sight.

It has been put, "God nothing does, nor suffers to be done, but what we would ourselves, could we but see through all events of things, as well as He." God did not promise we would miss the storms of life. He only promised that we would make the harbor at last.

Testing is the proof positive of genuine faith. In the early 1980's, I pastored in the metro area of Seattle. A member of the church was a retired employee of the airplane manufacturer, Boeing. He was involved in supervising employees who built many of the airplanes Boeing manufactured. I learned from him something about how airplanes are built. They start out by designing a rough sketch of a new plane on the drawing board. Then detailed blueprints begin to unfold and mock-up models are made. The models are tested in a variety of ways, and then initial construction begins with intricate and careful detail. After about two years the first plane will roll off the assembly line. The question still remains: Will it fly? Will it perform? Will it stand the test?

A test pilot must then put the plane through the paces in the air. This procedure is called stress testing. In aviation industry, such a procedure is required to identify the stall altitude of a passenger aircraft. It's a normal testing procedure. Other tests also involve load testing where an aircraft wing is bent to a ninety-degree angle to ensure that it does not develop any cracks in the fuselage. Don't worry! The aircraft would never take off like that once it comes into service! Recently, the new 737 Max aircraft produced by Boeing was tested taking off at a ninety degree angle – that's stress! So, when the aircraft has proven to be all that the maker has said it is and withstood all the testing, there is confidence in the plane to be built en masse and the airlines will then buy it. Finally, it is brought to the airport where passengers will board it and the plane thus becomes serviceable and useful. It's been tested.

In the same way, ore is brought to an assayer to prove that it is gold or silver. The assayer will put a fire under the raw ore and pour acid on it and then declares whether or not it is genuine – whether or not it is authentic.

Likewise, God puts our personal faith to the test to prove that it is genuine. It has been said that "the acid of grief tests the coin of belief." The aim of testing is not to destroy or afflict us, but to purge and refine. It is essential to Christian maturity. We are tested in order that God might produce patience in our lives.

Endurance means that we stand up under pressure. It involves a staying power that turns adversities of life into opportunities for growth. We cannot really know our depth of spiritual character until we see how we react under the pressures of life. Our difficult times in life should not make us bitter; they should make us better!

Many times our failure is in waiting for God to do his work in us. I call it a failure of faith. When we do not wait on God to respond or answer, we botch things up. We create problems for ourselves. We mess it up. We do not get it right.

That is why patience is an expression of the fruit of the Holy Spirit in our lives. You will never become more patient just by *trying* to be patient, but neither will the Holy Spirit place it on a silver platter and offer it to you as a gift. I have always said rather tongue-in-cheek that if you want patience, do not pray for it, because you will get a trial or tribulation! Something will happen that will remind you that you need to develop patience. Very simply, patience or perseverance comes through suffering and testing.

What effect does perseverance have in our life? The full effect of endurance is that it will make us mature, complete, and not lacking anything. Mature means that we are seasoned, experienced, well-developed, and fit for the tasks that God sent us into the world to do. William Barclay wrote, "By the way in which we meet every experience in life we are either fitting or unfitting ourselves for the task which God meant us to do."

Weaknesses and imperfections are being removed from our character. God does not want cheap substitutes; He wants thoroughly developed Christians.

More and more, as God works within us, we mirror Christ himself. We realize a contentment that comes from knowing God has what we need and when we need it. When we believe in God's faithfulness in our lives, we have everything we need. We will not be lacking anything!

None of us will always know how to handle the adversities or junk in our life. We will not have the wisdom we need to work through what happens to us. To receive the help we need to endure our trials so that our faith can be strengthened, we need to ask for wisdom – something God will freely give us, if only we ask Him. It is not as though God allows trials to come into our lives and then leaves us to our own devices. He will help us if we ask.

The fact is we need a certain kind of wisdom in order to consider it pure joy when we are faced with all kinds of difficulties in life. James echoes Proverbs 2:6-10, "The Lord gives wisdom; from his mouth come knowledge and understanding. He reserves ability for those with integrity. He is a shield for those who live a blameless life. He protects the paths of justice and guards the way of those who are loyal to him. Then you will understand righteousness and justice, as well as integrity, every good course. Wisdom will enter your mind, and knowledge will fill you with delight."

Wisdom is the God-given means by which we can discern the will of God, so that we know what it is that we are supposed to believe about God and His purposes in the midst of difficult times.

All of us need God's perspective to sustain us in suffering. It is a simple, but often difficult, promise to claim that God freely gives his wisdom to us whenever we ask him for it. We ask in faith – simply believing that when we ask for wisdom we have the expectation that we will be given that for which we ask.

You and I have trials, problems, troubles, and adversities, or just plain junk that happens to us in life. And some of us have a big trail of junk. How are you going to solve this problem? How are you going to meet this issue? How are you going to deal with this person? How are you going to clean up the junk? If you lack wisdom in regards to a problem, you need to ask God. You need not despair.

Wisdom is to know how to act under certain circumstances of testing, of trial, or when problems or questions arise. Life is filled, sometimes to the brim, with these and we need wisdom from God.

I have heard it and so have you. There are voices around you that teach you simply need to "pray and believe" and then everything will be alright for you. If you pray, believing that God will do something for you, he will do it if you just have enough faith. What happens when we believe we have enough faith and what we have prayed for just does not come to fruition? It is easy to view God as if he is some sort of wishing well or magic mirror or cosmic miracle wand. It is easy to think that if you can just wave a spiritual wand and believe, then you will get something. This teaching can easily lead us astray.

This is opposite of what James teaches us. The point James makes is that believers must pray *in* faith. Pray *in* faith! Our prayers must reflect confidence in God. And the confidence is not only in God's ability to give, but also confidence in God himself.

True wisdom is found, not in secular philosophy, or in personal experience, or in the communal judgment of any human culture, but in God. He alone is the Source of all true wisdom. It is to God that we must appeal if we desire it.

God is a giving God. Whatever God provides us is given generously. Our focus should not be on the *how much* of what God gives us, but on the basis that God gives to us without reluctance or hesitation. God does not give with a divided heart but freely and gladly. It is the same attitude we are to have when we give in return to God, for God loves (and is!) a cheerful giver (2 Corinthians 9:7).

God's generosity is universal. It is a basic characteristic of God revealed in the creation. Jesus himself guaranteed God's generosity to his children by reminding us that if we know how to give good gifts to our children, how much more our heavenly Father will give good gifts to those who ask him!

Nor does God scold or shame us for being needy in the first place. He gives to everyone without a second thought, without keeping score. God gives with no strings attached. He is not resentful of our dependence upon him. He welcomes our requests.

If we do not have wisdom that we need from God, it is simply because we have not asked for it. And since we are told that God will give us wisdom without a second thought, we know that this response from God our Father is a "pure, simple giving of good without a mixture of evil or bitterness" as Marvin Vincent puts it. Simply put, if we lack wisdom, and we do, we need to go to God. We must never hesitate but come boldly to God to get his wisdom.

It seems to me that the wisdom we are asking from God is the wisdom that we need in order to more fully understand what God is doing with us and for us in and through our suffering or adversity.

Asking a sufferer going through suffering to "ask in faith" can seem cruel, especially if the sufferer is at the end of the rope, and especially if we throw the "asking in faith" line at them in a self-righteous, flippant manner.

The solution is to ask in faith with no doubting. We need not look within at the strength of our faith or focus upon the difficulty of our circumstances. The key is to look carefully at the track-record of the One to whom we are asking for wisdom! It is not about you; it is about Him!

The opposite of asking in faith is identified as spiritual inconsistency and spiritual wavering, or "double-mindedness", as James calls it. This spiritual wavering comes from a fundamental uncertainty concerning God's existence, his goodness, his power, his love, or his trustworthiness. It produces an unwillingness on our part to place ourselves solely in His hands. Such a person is unstable in all their ways and is constantly vacillating between God and the world. The prayers which result are nothing more than empty words. Unsettled, going back and forth, driven by varying winds – that is the doubter's frame of mind.

It is much easier to keep from wavering spiritually if we keep before us the wonderful examples of the obedience of Jesus and the faithfulness of God in keeping his promises. God's answers to our troubles are not subject to the laws of probability and chance. God will always do what he says he will do. He simply requires our trust in Him.

The mere act of praying is not sufficient. It is necessary also that our heart be in accord with the request. God does not respond to "covering the bases" prayers, or "it couldn't hurt to pray" prayers, but only to prayers that reflect a wholehearted dependence and reliance on Him. It is not the *strength* or *intensity* of our belief that matters; it is the *clarity* and *simplicity* of our faith that matters.

How many times do we find ourselves wavering in our faith? Maybe we believe God is going to work it out, but then we jump at it ourselves and make our own decision about it. We think we have it all figured out. Or we turn a problem over to God and believe Him, but then the next moment or day we do not believe Him. We take it all back again. We decide that nothing has shown up by way of a solution or answer, so we go ahead and find a way to solve it ourselves, or so we think! This is where we make our mistake. When we respond in this way, we are just like the surf of the sea, tossed and turned by the wind.

Are you wondering how your problems are going to work out? Can you believe God? Can you trust God and turn them over to him?

Maybe trusting God is not your problem, but it too many times has been my problem. There have been places in my Christian walk when I simply have not believed God as I should have. I have not trusted Him as I should have. Indeed, I have trusted Christ as my Savior and received his grace and forgiveness and am assured of eternal life in heaven. Of that, I am confident as a child of God. But in this life, where the rubber meets the road, I have had my share of problems and adversities, just as you. My faith in God was put to the test and it was not always as resilient as it should have been.

At the death of my preacher father when he was but 50 years of age, my faith in God was sorely put to the test. I was a young pastor in my second year of pastoring, married, and starting a family with our first child, Chad, who was just one year old. I was pastoring my first church in Washington State and was far removed from family and many of my close friends.

It was a Saturday morning in summer 1982 when I received a phone call that my father was in the intensive care unit and in a coma in a Kansas City area hospital. At that moment, I felt as if the inside of my soul had been torn apart beyond any repair. I was overcome with fragile and vulnerable emotions that I was not even sure how to express them or how to say what I felt deeply inside. I was in indescribable emotional upheaval beyond words. I was stunned in horror.

On my quickly arranged airplane flight back to Kansas City that day, I was not sure my faith and confidence in God would endure. I was not sure it would hold – even though I had preached to everyone else to hold on to their faith – no matter what kind of junk that life throws at us.

I questioned the faithfulness of God, the goodness of God, and the justice of God. Why would God allow such a thing to happen to my father in the prime of life while pastoring a college campus church, leaving my mother a 46 year old widow with two of my siblings still at home? Why? There are no words to express the despairing grief that was in my deepest soul.

Here was one time in my life when I knew that I did not have the brains nor the spiritual survival skills to meet the trauma of life. It seemed more than I could bear. It was a time when my faith seemed to be ripped apart. It was a time when I knew I could do nothing more than ask God for wisdom beyond anything I could muster or for which I could hope – to help me get through this perplexing, confusing and fiery trial with the death of my father.

My prayer was one for faithfulness under trial. It was a prayer to endure in the face of the impending death of one whom I loved more than words could express. Too many times in my frail humanity, I found myself looking in all the wrong places for hope.

However, I discovered in those moments and in the years since that we are ultimately called to find hope in God's eternal promises. Looking back, I know with all certainty that when there is nothing else on which to hold, I can hold to God's unchanging hand. So can you.

Joy-filled is the person who endures with patience under trial. There is a pronouncement of blessing and powerful words of encouragement given to those facing difficult trials, even as I faced the premature death of my father. When we endure under trial and we stand the test, we are promised the crown of life.

I am reminded of the words of Fritz Rienecker who wrote, "A person who perseveres is one who bears up under something courageously and patiently. It is not the patience which can easily sit down and bow its head and let things descend upon it and passively endure until the storm is passed. It is the spirit which can bear things, not simply with resignation, but with a blazing hope."

While the prosperity gospel teaching and "name-it-and-claim-it" health and wealth theology has twisted the whole idea of being blessed and having faith out of its context, the reality is that we are indeed promised God's blessing when we faithfully endure our trials. But it is not always the blessing we might think it would be. We are promised courage to face difficult choices and events in life and overcome adversity when we choose the way of Christ. It is not a blind faith or a blind hope.

What we have to do is gain a perspective that helps us look beyond our current circumstances to what ultimately lies ahead. God never promises to end our struggles, but he does promise to reward those who endure them faithfully.

I am reminded of the lyrics written by William Hunter in the classic hymn entitled *Is Not This the Land of Beulah*? Hunter pens the words, "Tell me not of heavy crosses, nor of burdens hard to bear. For I've found this great salvation, makes each burden light appear. And I love to follow Jesus, gladly counting all but dross, worldly honors all forsaking, for the glory of the cross." How very true!

The powerful image of being promised a crown is quite reassuring. The idea of receiving a crown of life (here in James the word means "a laurel-wreath") is one drawn from the athletic field of the Greek Olympic games. It was a head wreath, the victor's prize in the Greek games. It might also be given to the person whom the public wished to honor and it was worn in religious and secular feasts.

Like an athlete, the Christian must strive to complete the race, persevere in spiritual training, and endure the trials that will bring maturity and completeness to faith. In the end, there is a crown.

The way to get into God's winner's circle is to love Him and stay faithful, even under the pressures of life. In this case, the crown is the blessing of eternal life. Those who endure will be blessed with a kind of life beyond anything we can imagine. The things of life will grow strangely dim in the light of his glory and grace.

There is a finish line. The trials of life are contained in this life. Someday the tests and troubles of life will be over. In the end, what matters is not whether our testing has been difficult or easy for us in life. What matters is whether we have been approved by God through the tests.

We are all faced with the race of life. God offers to help us along the way. What we do not know about this life is how long our personal race will be, nor do we know what obstacles we will meet along the way. We are simply reminded to run the race of life with finishing on our minds – whatever it takes to do so. And our dependence on God must be unwavering, filled with holy courage and constant.

At the end of the day, the solution to the problem of the suffering of believers is one of perspective. In ways we cannot fully grasp in the present moment, God will indeed use the troubles of life to strengthen our faith, to make us strong and steadfast, and to bring his work in us to its ultimate goal.

Since God has begun this work in us by giving us life, God will see his work through to completion. How do we know that? Because God has promised to do this and because he is the giver of every good and perfect gift. He will give us all that we need. All that he asks of us is that we ask him for what we need in faith and that we do not doubt. And we can only ask in faith without doubting if we see our gracious and grace-filled God as the giver of all good and perfect gifts. As we love God, his promises become ours. And whatever junk life may throw at us, we will still have joy – from the inside, out.

Putting this into practice will enable us to live the 24/7 life.

Words to Live by from the Church Fathers

ORIGIN: *If you count it all joy when you fall into various temptations, you give birth to joy, and you offer that joy in sacrifice to God.*

CHRYSOSTOM: *For in the world there is no one who wins a trophy without suffering, who has not strengthened himself with labors and dieting and exercise and vigils and many other things like that. How much more is that true in this battle!*

OECUMENIUS: *Why do trials produce patience? It is because trials demonstrate the purity of faith, which is made perfect by the patient endurance of affliction.*

BEDE: *Patience builds character, so that someone who possesses it cannot be overcome but is shown to be perfect. For this reason believers are tested in order to improve their patience, so that by it their faith may be seen to be perfect.*

AUGUSTINE: *Just because faith may be given to us before we ask for it, it does not follow that it is not a gift of God. God may well give it to us before we ask him for it, just as he also gives peace and love. This is why we pray both that faith may be increased in those who already have it and also that it may be given to those who have not yet received it.*

SULPICIUS SEVERUS: *Disasters are the common lot of the saints, who must suffer them. It is by enduring them and overcoming them that the virtue of the righteous has always been noticeable. With invincible strength they have defied all trials – the heavier the sufferings they endured, the more courageous were their victories.*

3

KICKING TEMPTATION IN THE TEETH
James 1:13-18

"No one who is tested should say, "God is tempting me!" This is because God is not tempted by any form of evil, nor does he tempt anyone." (James 1:13)

Mark Antony was known as the silver-throated orator of Rome. He was also credited with being a brilliant man, a strong leader and a courageous soldier. But one thing he lacked was strength of character. On the outside, he was impressive and magnificent. On the inside, he was weak and vulnerable. This so enraged his tutor that on one occasion he shouted at him, "O Marcus! O colossal child! You are able to conquer the world but unable to resist a temptation!"

That indictment fits not only Mark Antony, but too many people today. No one is immune to the bewitching appeals of temptation's sirens. And some, like Antony, find it virtually impossible to resist the pull of the alluring voices of temptation.

James began this letter by addressing the problem of trials. We know that a trial is an ordeal, a hardship, something that puts our faith to the test. We know also that we must have a correct view of God in order to persevere during times of trial.

But we also need to understand God's view of our temptations. Trials and temptations are always with us and present us with a myriad of choices. However, they are not one and the same.

Many people think that the presence of trials indicates the presence of sin, but nothing could be further from the truth. There is nothing inherently immoral or sinful about experiencing a trial, as we can see from the lives of a few well-known Bible characters and heroes of faith.

Job faced excruciating losses in practically every area of his life (Job 1-2). Yet we are told that in all of this, Job did not sin by blaming God (Job 1:22). He asked the aged question, "Will we receive good from God but not also receive bad? In all this, Job didn't sin with his lips" (Job 2:10). Elijah experienced deep depression when his life was threatened (1 Kings 19). And the apostle John, when he was banished to the island of Patmos faced a test of loneliness (Revelation 1:9). In each case, the trial was brought on by a particular set of circumstances, not by sin.

Temptations, however, are different from trials. Trials and hardships come from without. They are an inevitable part of living in a fallen, sin-cursed world. Hardships can produce spiritual maturity and lead to eternal benefits when they are endured in faith.

When we fail the test we give in to temptation. Temptations spring from within us when we are tempted by our own cravings. Whereas the end of trials is growth, the end of temptation is death.

When we fail we use all kinds of excuses and reasons for our actions. The most dangerous of the reasons or excuses that we use is that of blaming God for tempting us. It is with this in mind that James talks to us about temptation and its progression in our lives.

It is important for us to understand how James uses the word tempt or temptation. It is a word that stands for a direct impulse which can result in an evil response. So, we can be assured that God does not tempt people for evil. God is not the origin of our temptations. Temptation to sin is the operation of evil forces and the devil.

It is not a matter of *if* we are tempted, but *when* we are tempted. When tempted we remember that temptation is inevitable in life. The moment we entered this world we were drafted into a lifelong battle with temptation. The monk living behind the monastery walls struggles with it just like the person who works in a busy downtown office.

As followers of Christ, we are not blamed for having to ward off temptations. None of us can eradicate the presence of these enticements that come our way. But we are responsible for our reactions to them.

God does not work at cross-purposes with himself. He does not call us to persevere while at the same time setting up spiritual stumbling blocks or roadblocks in our path. While God does in fact allow tests and trials into our lives, their purpose is to reveal and strengthen our faith, not to undermine or destroy it. God does not entice anyone to sin; he does not set traps for our souls and lure us into them, nor does the Holy Spirit ever speak to our hearts, calling us away from God.

Temptation to sin arises within us because we have a nature that can be prone to sin and easily wanders, not because God somehow tempts us to sin. What this means in practical terms is simply this: you cannot blame God for your sin no matter how difficult your circumstances. If you surrender to the temptation to sin, the devil did not make you do it. It is not the other person's fault. It is not that you couldn't help it. It is not that everybody's doing it. It was not just a mistake. It is not that nobody's perfect. It is not that you didn't know it was wrong. It was not that you were pressured into it. Those are simply excuses that seek to shift blame from the real culprit.

We are surrounded by a culture of blame shifting. We blame one another. We blame our circumstances. We blame the way in which we are made – all for the sins of which we are guilty.

This kind of blame shifting is clearly rebuked – that it is always somebody else's fault. When we sin, when we yield to temptation, it is our own choice. To God, it is a person's own desires or cravings to sin that is the culprit.

Because God's character is holy, pure, and totally separate from sin, he cannot be involved in sin. When temptation enters our lives, we are solely responsible for how we respond to it. We make a conscious decision to act upon those desires. And our actions, when sinful, earn for us the appropriate wage, death. So, while God allows trials to come our way, God does not tempt us to sin.

God cannot be tempted by evil. This means that God is not in any sense the author of evil or temptation. God does not wish evil on people. He does not cause evil. He does not try to trip people up. God never induces us to sin nor does he try to destroy our faith.

For God to draw us into sin would be contrary to his own character. Since he himself cannot be tempted to sin, he has no interest in influencing us to do evil. Statements in the

Old Testament that the Israelites "tempted" God (see Psalm 78:41) indicate that they provoked and angered God by their disobedience, not that there was something in God's nature which could have caused him to respond unrighteously.

On the contrary, God promises always to provide "a way out" so that we are never tempted beyond our ability to bear. He provides a way to resist temptation. "No temptation has seized you that isn't common for people. But God is faithful. He won't allow you to be tempted beyond your abilities. Instead, with the temptation, God will also supply a way out so that you will be able to endure it" (1 Corinthians 10:13).

In my pastoral ministry across the years, I have had many of my parishioners ask me the question, "If God really loves us, then why doesn't he protect us from temptation?" I believe that the simple answer to that question is that a God who keeps us from temptation is a God that is unwilling to let us grow in our faith.

Temptation is an individual matter. Temptation comes from within. James highlights individual responsibility for sin.

Like metal to a magnet, the desires of the heart can be drawn to temptation. But nothing outside of ourselves, no person, force or set of circumstances nor any allurement, is strong enough in itself to compel us or force us to sin. We make the choice.

William Barclay wrote that "sin would be helpless if there was nothing in human beings to which it could appeal. Desire is something which can be nourished or stifled. It can be controlled and even, by the grace of God, eliminated if dealt with at once. But people can allow their thoughts to follow certain tracks, and their steps to take them into certain places and their eyes to linger on certain things, and so stimulate desire . . . . it is undisciplined minds and uncommitted hearts that are vulnerable. If someone encourages desire for long enough, there is an inevitable consequence. Desire becomes action."

In short, desires can be fed or starved. If the desire itself is evil, we must deny its wish within our heart and mind. The kind of desire James is describing is desire that is out of control. It is selfish and seductive desire.

The responsibility for our susceptibility to temptation lies within our own hearts. An opportunity or invitation to sin will produce no result unless it is met with desire and a willingness to transgress God's commands in order to obtain the thing desired. Only then can an external source of temptation evoke the internal, subjective response of yielding to it. The progression from desire to sin, and eventually to spiritual death, is a slippery slope.

Throughout his letter, James uses metaphors to create word pictures for his readers. He uses the metaphor of wind-tossed waves (James 1:6), and withering plants (James 1:10-11). When James talks about temptation, he chooses to use the imagery of fish bait.

He expresses the lure of temptation in two ways – being dragged away or being lured like a fish to bait and then being enticed.

Temptation that leads to sin always follows the same process.

First, the bait is dropped. We can be hooked by a temptation like a fish by bait because we are hungry – hungry for the fulfillment of our legitimate physical, emotional and spiritual needs. God promises to provide for those needs, but Satan also knows about our hungers. And although he cannot force us to eat, Satan is a skilled angler at knowing when, where, and how to drop bait in our path to lure us away from God and righteous living. It is the evil one who tempts us to fulfill legitimate desires in illegitimate ways.

Then, inner desire is attracted to the bait. It is expressed by James with the use of the word enticement. The word entice is actually a fishing term.

We all know that a hook baited with light bulbs will not catch any fish! In order to pull a fish from its comfortable hiding place, one has to find a bait that will interest it and even one that cannot be resisted. Once the bait is dropped and the fish sees it, a fisherman will tell you that it is as good as caught.

The more we seek God's kingdom and his righteousness, and the more we draw from him our strength and our delight, the less we will be interested in the tempting, illegitimate bait that is continually dropped around us.

All desire in itself is not sin, but it becomes so when indulged in beyond the point at which satisfying the desire would mean stepping outside the boundaries of God's revealed will. When that line is crossed, whether in overt deeds or only in the heart, sin takes root and begins to grow.

Sin occurs when we yield to ungodly temptations. When we allow these temptations to join the desires within the womb of our mind and heart, it gives birth to sin. The desire is joined to the will. The desiring and the conceiving emphasize the internal nature of sin.

Thomas a Kempis, an Early Church father wrote, "At first it [temptation] is a mere thought confronting the mind; then imagination paints it in strong colors; only after that do we take pleasure in it, and the will makes a false move, and we give assent."

Desires that present themselves to us in expressions that begin with "I have to have," "I can't do without," or even "I would do anything if only I could" are all ripe for conception and birth into sin, when they are illegitimate desires and wrongful expressions in our lives. It is helpful to ask ourselves occasionally, "What reasoning do I use that tends to lead me into sin?"

Sin is full-blown and gives birth to spiritual death when it becomes a fixed habit in our life and a pattern of living. Spiritual death is separation from God.

Even though sin sometimes brings a temporary period of pleasure, it always spawns consequences. Satan tries to blur our vision to these consequences by intoxicating us with the wine of pleasure or gain. But that pleasure has a high cost of hurt to ourselves, to others, and to Christ.

We are called to "avoid worldly desires that wage war against your lives" (1 Peter 2:11). Similarly, Proverbs 4:23 cautions, "More than anything you guard, protect your mind, for life flows from it. "

We are called to counteract temptation, not tolerate it. We are called to actively resist sin, not passively embrace it. If certain kinds of music, magazines, visuals, or habits bring before you alluring images and temptations, then by allowing them in your life you are not counteracting sin and temptation. You are tolerating it. How often do we pray for deliverance from some temptation only to turn around and expose ourselves to it?

It has been said, "To pray against temptations, and yet to rush into occasions, is to thrust your fingers into the fire, and then pray they might not be hurt."

We are called to use the right resistance. The method of resistance must match the temptation. Not all temptations can be handled in the same way. For example, every time sensual or sexual sins are mentioned in the New Testament, we are told to flee, to run, to get away. For the one who wrestles with the temptation to get rich, the Scriptures teach that you can subdue it by being generous (1 Timothy 6:9-10, 17-19). If your living or working environment is laden with temptations, Proverbs 4:25 gives a practical suggestion to put the leash of self-control on your wandering eyes to keep them looking straight ahead.

Although our tactics of resistance to temptation may vary as we go through different seasons of our life, we must never be lulled into feeling we have arrived at some spiritual plateau and are no longer vulnerable to temptation.

We are called to remind ourselves that the final pain of giving in to temptation to sin will erase the temporary pleasure.

Do you remember how you love to dip your finger into the chocolate icing before it goes on the cake? And how that rich, sugary concoction convinces you that you are going to die if you don't eat all of it in the bowl? And how after you have sneaked out on the back porch and eaten the whole thing, you wish you could die because your stomach hurts due to your overdose of delicious chocolate and your taste that could somehow not wait?

We can all identify with suffering the consequences of our temptations to give in, whether it is as simple as eating a bowl of chocolate icing or doing something much more serious and with far greater consequences in life.

We must cultivate in ourselves the same faith that guarded Moses. "By faith Moses refused to be called the son of Pharaoh's daughter when he was grown up. He chose to be mistreated with God's people instead of having the temporary pleasures of sin" (Hebrews 11:24-25).

We are not to be deceived about God's goodness and about the source of temptation. We will battle temptation on a daily basis. Some temptations are stronger than others and will be more easily defeated than others.

But just because you successfully resist a particular temptation does not mean that you have conquered it forever. Temptation often comes whispering and over time it gradually erodes our will to resist.

C.S. Lewis, in his book *The Screwtape Letters*, cleverly exposes this subtlety through a fictitious letter written by an older devil named Screwtape, to his young nephew, named Wormwood. He writes:

"My Dear Wormwood, Obviously you are making excellent progress. My only fear is lest in attempting to hurry the patient you awaken him to a sense of his real position. For you and I, who see that position as it really is, must never forget how totally different it ought to appear to him. We know that we have introduced a change of direction in his course which is already carrying him out of his orbit around the Enemy [God]; but he must be made to imagine that all the choices which have effected this change of course are trivial and revocable. He must not be allowed to suspect that he is now, however slowly, heading right away from the sun on a line which will carry him into the cold and dark of utmost space."

Remember Mark Antony? Go back to his story again. As the story goes, Mark Antony's most widely known and costly temptation floated to him on a barge. Bedecked as a dazzling bait, Cleopatra sailed up the Cydnus River straight into the unguarded heart of Mark Antony. Their adulterous relationship with its passing pleasure cost him his wife, his place as a world leader, and ultimately his life. Manipulated by Cleopatra into believing she was dead, this "colossal child" fell on his sword, committing suicide out of devotion to what was once only a temptation and something that could have been avoided.

How true it is. We commit spiritual suicide when we give in to something that could have been avoided and we reap the end result. While we are free to choose, we are never free to choose the consequences.

Believing in God is important, but it also matters how we believe in God. We are all capable of believing in God – the wrong way. It is this very deception of believing in God the wrong way that James attacks throughout his letter.

So, how is it that we can keep from falling into temptation? Rather than being the source of temptation or evil, God is in fact the source of every good thing and of every blessing in our lives. Every good and perfect gift comes from him. We can always be assured that God wills the best for us –

not good things today and bad things tomorrow. Whatever happens is for our best. God's gifts are always good.

He is the Creator of the heavenly lights – the sovereign Creator who demonstrates his providential care over all his creation, including the sun, moon, and stars (Genesis 1:14-16; Psalm 136:7-9). Just as he upholds them, so also he sustains us, as well as all plant and animal life, and he reigns over all the forces of nature upon which our lives depend (Job 38:1-39:30).

And God does not change like shifting shadows. Unlike the heavenly bodies, which are in constant change and motion, God is the same from eternity past to eternity future. Neither his character nor his purposes change; He is the timeless "I AM" (Exodus 3:13-14). Thus, his promises will certainly be fulfilled and his goodness toward us will never cease.

It is a healthy spiritual exercise for us to express our gratefulness to God for his unchanging love towards us.

There is a reason why we express our gratefulness to God. That is because "He chose to give us birth by his true word and here is the result: we are like the first crop from the harvest of everything he created" (James 1:18).

I love this expression and imagery given by James. It reminds us of the Old Testament teaching. The Old Testament taught Jews to bring their "first crops," or the first and best of their harvests as an offering to God (Exodus 34:22).

The greatest example of God giving good things is the gift of salvation through the Living Word, Jesus Christ, with the gift of eternal life (Ephesians 1:13). Believers are first-crops because we are a new creation in Christ. We are no longer sinners separated from God, but God's own children (Romans 8:19-23). Our new birth in Christ, by which we are made a new creation, is only the first of many good things to come in the new heavens and new earth (2 Peter 3:13).

Since we are chosen by God, we are called to live as examples of God's goodness and role models of what he can do in our lives. Jesus, in his own words, reminds us that we are the salt and light in a decaying, dark, confused and broken world. We are called to make this our passionate and consuming desire. We have been brought to faith in Christ so that we will become the down-payment on what will eventually happen to all of creation – God will remove the curse.

As Paul expresses it, "We know that the whole creation is groaning together and suffering labor pains up until now. And it's not only creation. We ourselves who have the Spirit as the first crop of the harvest also groan inside as we wait to be adopted and for our bodies to be set free" (Romans 8:22-23).

The word of truth from God, which brought forth the first creation, now brings about our regeneration through the Holy Spirit.

And when we are given new life through the Holy Spirit, we understand in new and living ways the priority of living our lives 24/7, true to our faith in Jesus Christ.

Words to Live by from the Church Fathers

AUGUSTINE: *Because we are human, we live a most dangerous life amid the snares of temptation.*

BEDE: *Nobody will take the disciples' joy from them because, although they suffered persecution and torture on behalf of Christ's name, yet they willingly bore all adversities because they were enkindled by hope in his resurrection and by their vision of him. Moreover, they thought it perfect joy when they encountered different kinds of temptations.*

SYMEON THE NEW THEOLOGIAN: *The Word of God . . . causes us to despise all life's painful experiences and to count as joy every trial that assails us.*

THEOPHYLACT: *Humility is the distributor of all good things, and apart from it there is nothing which is good.*

HESYCHIUS: *The desires of sinners are the birth pangs of death.*

CYRIL OF JERUSALEM: *If we ever find ourselves afflicted by illness, grief, or trouble, let us not blame God, for God cannot be tempted by evil and does not tempt anyone. Each of us is scourged by the ropes of our own sins.*

AUGUSTINE: *The one giving birth is lust, the thing born is sin. Lust does not give birth unless it conceives, and it does not conceive unless it entices and receives willing consent to commit evil. Therefore our battle against lust consists in keeping it from conceiving and giving birth to sin.*

4

MIRROR, MIRROR IN THE WORD
James 1:19-27

"Those who hear but don't do the word are like those who look at their faces in a mirror." (James 1:23)

Snow White and the Seven Dwarfs is a Walt Disney classic fairytale – a favorite among children and I think among adults, too. You know the story.

Once upon a time there lived a lovely princess with fair skin and blue eyes. She was so fair that she was named Snow White. Her mother died when Snow White was a baby and her father married again. This queen was very pretty but she was also very cruel. The wicked stepmother wanted to be the most beautiful lady in the kingdom and she would often ask her magic mirror, "Mirror! Mirror on the wall! Who is the fairest of them all?" And the magic mirror would say, "You are, Your Majesty!" But one day, the mirror replied, "Snow White is the fairest of them all!" The wicked queen was very angry and jealous of Snow White. And, well, you know the rest of the story.

There is another mirror that is far more important than any mirror on the wall of your house. It is what James calls the "mirror of God's Word." James calls us to see ourselves in the mirror of God's Word, listen to the message of truth and then live a life consistent with that message. In short, our walk needs to match our talk.

Maybe you recall that the apostle Paul wrote two letters in the New Testament to Timothy, his son in the faith. He reminded Timothy (2 Timothy 3:13), and now us, that we are to obey the word of God. And he makes clear the reason. All Scripture is inspired by God and is useful for teaching (what is right), for showing people what is wrong in their lives (what is not right), for correcting faults (how to get right), and for teaching how to live right (how to stay right). Using the Scriptures, the person who serves God will be capable, having all that is needed to do every good work.

So, we know the word of God that brings us life also has the power to guide us in living the life it has brought us. And we are now offered some really practical down-to-earth essentials for what that might look like in our life.

As a starting point, it is an interesting list that James compiles for us in James 1. It is a list about the things in which it is best to be quick and the things in which it is best to be slow.

It is always good to listen well before we speak. In fact, we are reminded that we need to be *quick to listen*. The scholar F.J.A. Hort says that those who are really good will be much more anxious to listen to God than arrogantly, loudly and stridently to shout their own opinions. Zeno of Elea said, "We have two ears but only one mouth, that we may hear more and speak less." Many have demonstrated the truth of the saying by Laurence Peter: "Speak when you're angry, and you'll give the best speech you'll ever regret."

In contrast to the power and purity of God's word, our words are often ill-considered, overly harsh and riddled with misunderstanding and half-truths. So, we must weigh our words carefully. What feels like righteous indignation may be nothing more than self-centered bile.

The ease and availability of social media in our culture presents a special challenge. It is all too easy to fire off a note without reflection, letting our passions dictate the tone and content. Who among us has not regretted hitting the send button on an e-mail, a fraction of a second too late? Or maybe you have had more than one regret about some Facebook tirade, rant or comment that did nothing more than bring insult to your own character or someone else's character.

Things are not always as they first appear. When we pause to listen before drawing conclusions it can save us from responding in a way that is destructive to relationships. So it is that we should be quick (eager and willing) to hear what others have to say. We should be quick and willing to consider alternative explanations and points of view. How much different things would be in our lives if this were our consistent way of living.

Certainly, we need to be more ready to listen to what God says than to intrude our own ideas and opinions. We are called to be *slow to speak*. We have two ears and one mouth. It reminds us that we should listen more than we speak. And it is especially so when it comes to God's word. We are to check what we hear with God's Word. If we do not listen both carefully and quickly, we risk being led into all kinds of false teaching and error. Listening is a virtue. As Christians we must cultivate the grace of sympathetic listening before we respond.

I have discovered that wisdom is the ability to restrain our responses. Why do we think we have to respond to everything that is said or every reaction we see? Sometimes the best wisdom is simply remaining silent, listening carefully, considering prayerfully, and then if speak is needed, speaking quietly. I suggest that is often the best wisdom when it comes to our responses.

If you have ever been around someone who talked too much and listened too little, you have discovered that the message they send is that *their ideas* are more important than *yours*. And that is an annoying conversation when it befalls you.

Exhortations of a similar nature are found throughout James, suggesting that intemperate speech was an area of sin for the recipients of the letter (see James 1:26, 3:1-12, 4:11-12). And, I might add, it is an area of sin for too many of us. This is not surprising, since suffering and persecution, if not received with a godly attitude (James 1:2-3), can easily produce interpersonal conflict and angry outbursts.

This theme is also found throughout Scripture. The ability to master one's tongue and temper is viewed, not merely as a desirable character trait, but also as an indication of spiritual maturity and wisdom.

Proverbs 17:27, 28 teaches us: "Wise are those who restrain their talking; people with understanding are coolheaded. Fools who keep quiet are deemed wise; those who shut their lips are smart." How often is it in our lives when we would do well to simply restrain our talking? It has been rightly observed that the tongue is in a moist place and slips too easily!

It is James' advice that we should be *slow to anger*. In general, anger does not produce God-honoring conduct; in fact, quite the opposite. It is more frequently associated with such acts as slander, murder, and bitter quarrels (Matthew 5:21-26; James 4:1-3).

And even though this truth to be *slow to anger* is stated without qualification, there are some exceptions when anger expresses itself towards injustice and sin. When injustice and sin occur, we *should* become angry because others are being hurt, degraded and destroyed.

Take a look at the story of Jesus in Mark 3. Jesus was in the synagogue on the Sabbath and noticed a man with a deformed hand. Jesus' enemies were watching him closely. They were there to see if Jesus would heal the man's hand on the Sabbath, so they could condemn Jesus for healing on the Sabbath, a no-no in their day. Jesus' question to his enemies was rather pointed. "Is it legal on the Sabbath to do good or to do evil, to save life or to kill?" (Mark 3:4). They had no answer. And we are told that Jesus looked around at them with anger, because he was deeply grieved at their unyielding hearts. At Jesus' request the man reached out his hand and was healed. Why was Jesus angry?

It can be said that Jesus was angry for the right reasons. The truth of his life and testimony was being rejected by those who were trying to know him best. Jesus was angry at hearts that would not yield to his ways and his truth. This was not an anger of vengeance, but an anger that truth was being rejected – truth that can change lives.

The anger that is forbidden is a thoughtless, uncontrolled temper that leads to rash, hurtful words. Think about all the places where anger can erupt.

As a pastor for over 38 years, I have seen rash and hurtful anger erupt in churches, when church members feel unnoticed, overlooked, unappreciated or criticized. Our evening news reports are full of stories where anger erupted in the workplace, because some employee was slighted, overworked, harassed, or criticized. Anger erupts among friends, when someone feels left out, disappointed or criticized. Anger wedges its devilish hand into family relationships, creating estrangement. And we know that anger erupts in violent and destructive ways in our culture every day.

I recall an incident in one church where I pastored. I was leading a church business meeting and the congregation was seeking to make a decision about a capital improvement project on the church facilities. Everyone was being given an opportunity to voice their opinion and idea. As people were taking turns speaking, I detected one person who was visibly getting agitated about what was being shared. Finally, without waiting for my acknowledgement for him to speak, the person interrupted and began an angry tirade about everything that he thought was wrong, attacking others viewpoints and ideas. He reached his boiling point when he could no longer speak due to his anger, abruptly and loudly left the sanctuary shouting in anger, slammed the sanctuary exit door as he left, and roared away peeling the tire cars in the gravel parking lot adjacent to the church. His anger was made known to all in rather dramatic ways! It was thoughtless and uncontrolled temper.

We are living in a ferociously angry world where people's emotions are stretched to uncontrollable dimensions. It cannot be denied that expressed anger most often tends to be uncontrollable and wreaks havoc, and sadly, tragically, even death. It should be easy to understand that this kind of anger does not produce the kind of life within us and others that God desires.

To be quick to listen, slow to speak, and slow to anger is the way to live life 24/7. It makes a clear statement about the way we choose to live. This is the kind of living that will make a difference to people around us.

As followers of Christ we are always called to act differently. We are called upon to get rid of all moral filth and receive with humility the word of God. Since we have experienced the new birth, we are called to purge from our lives any conduct which is inconsistent with it.

James also uses a powerful imagery about getting rid of something in our lives. The imagery of the phrase "get rid of" that James uses is one of stripping off a set of dirty clothing. It implies that such things are no longer an essential part of us, but something external to be removed and discarded – just like we would take off dirty clothes at the end of a day and choose not to wear them again until they have been washed clean.

We are called to set aside all moral filth and the growth of wickedness in our lives. We are then called to welcome the word planted deep inside us – the very word that is able to save us.

This is one of the main themes of James. When we choose to receive or accept the word of God it requires more than merely agreeing with it intellectually. Active obedience to the word is required. We must do what it says, otherwise, we have not truly accepted it at all, but are only engaged in self-deception. God's word directs us in identifying and removing those things that are unacceptable in our life. His Word and His Spirit also work inside us. Whatever happens to us in spiritual growth happens from the inside out.

The response of our faith is to purify ourselves, through the Spirit of Christ, from the immorality and evil which surrounds us and suffuses our culture.

For the believer, the word is not merely *external* (something we hear or read), but *internal* (something we receive). It has been planted within us through the presence of the indwelling Holy Spirit (Romans 8:9, 11).

The command to accept the word of God is not a call to conversion. It is a call to submit to the ongoing influence of the Spirit as he applies God's word to our lives (Galatians 5:16, 25). As the implanted word of God becomes part of us, we absorb the characteristics taught in the word and these are to be expressed in our living. That is when we walk the talk. That is when we live the life. That is when we live the 24/7 kind of life.

And here is what happens to us. It will save our souls. When we talk about saving our souls, we are talking about the future aspect of our salvation, our final transformation and glorification at the return of Christ (1 Corinthians 15:50-54).

Justification is an event in the past, sanctification is both an event (being set apart by God for his purposes) and a process (becoming progressively more like Christ in our daily experience), and glorification is yet to come. So, the word of God implanted in our hearts has the power to ensure that the work which God began in us in the past (our justification), and which he is now continuing in the present (our sanctification), will certainly be brought to completion in the future (our glorification).

And as if that isn't enough to talk to us about how we talk and listen and respond, there is some more hard-hitting truth in James.

In classic back-to-his-theme form, James gives us a no-holds-barred command. We are called to be a *doer of the word* and not just a *hearer of the word* only! In short, do what the word says to do! Live it.

Too many people have the mistaken idea that hearing a good message or Bible study is what makes them grow and receive God's blessing. It is not the *hearing* of God's word that brings the blessing. It is the *doing* of God's word that brings the blessing. God's word does not profit us anything if we do not do what it says. We learn God's Word not just to know it, but also to do it.

If you think you are spiritual because you go to church, or because you are a member, or because you give, or because you have been around spiritual things all of your life, you are wrong. In fact, you are deceiving yourself.

Believing you are something you are not simply because you know the facts or the truth of God's word is self-deception. It is self-deception to congratulate yourself about knowledge of Scripture if that is all there is to your spiritual life.

It is too easy to substitute reading for doing or talking for doing! It was Bruce Barton who said, "Passive Christianity is morally wrong." God's word can only grow in the soil of obedience.

I have already reminded you about the fairy tale of Walt Disney lore. That one about the "mirror, mirror on the wall. Who's the fairest of them all." Well, here we have what I call this "mirror, mirror in the word."

God's word is compared to a mirror. It shows us what we really are. We need to see ourselves as God sees us. The call to do what the word of God says to do lies at the core of our spiritual life. Put into practice what you say you believe.

There are two basic ways you can evaluate your physical appearance. One is to look in a mirror and observe yourself or you can look at a photograph of yourself.

You and I both know that a photographer can work miracles on a photo. A photographer does things no one else can do for you. Blemishes can be removed, a touch-up here and there, shade in the light spots, cover the wrinkles on the face – well, generally the photographer can make us look quite presentable to those we want to show the photo. Basically, a photo can be quite flattering of our appearance. The photographer deals with us in mercy; not justice. No offense to the photographer, but the truth is that the photographer with the camera is not as honest as the other option – a mirror.

When you see yourself in a mirror, it cannot be denied that the view in the mirror is absolutely and brutally honest. It reveals your true image. It shows you exactly what you look like at that moment. It shows you exactly as you are at that moment.

When I arise in the morning I see my face in the mirror and I am confronted with all the corrective work that needs to be done before I present myself the world. At that moment, a mirror reveals who I truly am and not who I would like to think I am. If I simply walk away from the mirror and forget what I see, I may be fooling myself but certainly no one else in the world is fooled. Everyone knows what I look like and can recognize me for who I actually am – not for who I think I am. It cannot be denied.

So it is with the mirror of God's word. It points to all our strengths and weaknesses. Unless we heed its instructions, unless we make the necessary corrections in our lives, we are nothing more than spiritual phonies. We may be *talking about* the word, but we are not *walking by* the word.

To look at our reflection in a mirror and then forget what we have seen, to walk away without making any adjustment, such as combing our hair or adjusting our tie, would be pointless.

It is equally senseless and pointless for us to hear the word but then fail to respond to it by altering our behavior and make no changes in our life. And yet in a spiritual sense, people do this repeatedly. They hear a sermon or read a Bible passage that reveals something about themselves, but choose to ignore it rather than act upon it. What difference has it made in their life? Does anyone even notice anything distinctively different?

Too often we mouth the correct confessions of our faith and we master the orthodox theology of our faith, but our faith is still dead – without works. Proclaiming the faith on Sunday morning is good. Living the faith Monday through Sunday is far better. Our faith has to be 24/7.

God's word does something a mirror cannot do. It not only reveals what we need, but also points us to the remedy and the correction. It shows us what is wrong and how to fix it. When God's word shows something within us that needs correction, we are called to listen and act.

James echoes the message of Christ, who said, "Happy rather are those who hear God's word and put it into practice" (Luke 11:28). Likewise, Jesus taught that "those who don't put into practice what they hear are like a person who built a house without a foundation. The floodwater smashed against it and it collapsed instantly. It was completely destroyed" (Luke 6:49).

The danger that James (and Jesus) warns against is insidious and real. It is the danger of equating knowledge with life and theory with reality.

What kind of self-deception is this? Self-deception is convincing ourselves that we know God when in fact we know only about him. Self-deception is persuading ourselves that we have spiritual life when we possess only the appearance of it. Such is the condition of those who listen to the word, who read, study, discuss, and even preach it, but who fail to submit to it in practice.

I know the idea that a person can be mistaken about whether they have come to know God is disturbing and hard to accept. And yet the Scriptures are clear that our intuitive judgments concerning even our own spiritual condition are not infallible.

So, Paul exhorts us, "Examine yourselves to see if you are in the faith. Test yourselves. Don't you understand that Jesus Christ is in you? Unless, of course, you fail the test" (2 Corinthians 13:5).

The test is whether our conduct is consistent with our profession of faith. Likewise, Jesus states, "Not everybody who says to me 'Lord, Lord,' will get into the kingdom of heaven. Only those who do the will of my Father who is in heaven will enter. On the Judgement Day, many people will say to me, 'Lord, Lord, didn't we prophesy in your name, and expel demons in your name drive out demons and do lots of miracles in your name? Then I'll tell them, 'I've never known you. Get away from me, you people who do wrong.'" (Matthew 7:21-23). Pretty serious truth I would say. Whether we read God's word or hear it read, our listening must result in an attitude of submission that leads to obedience.

Step back for a moment and think about faith and works in the Christian life – a basic and core message of the Book of James. The necessity of obedience in the life of the believer seems to imply that justification is by works, rather than by faith. But this reverses the sequence of events. Our good works do not cause or merit our salvation; only the work of Christ on the cross can do that.

Instead, works (as practiced in a holy and obedient life) are always the *result* of the salvation which Christ accomplishes for and in us. So, if a professing Christian is indifferent to the claims of Christ on his or her life it casts doubt upon the reality of the faith they claim to have.

When we make changes in our life in active response to God's word, what are we really doing? We are looking intently into the perfect law of liberty that gives us freedom as followers of Christ.

Since James' readers were primarily ethnic Jews, we might conclude that he is making reference to the Old Testament law. However, the Old Testament legal code (*Torah*) is never portrayed in the New Testament as bringing freedom; in fact, just the opposite is true. That law is viewed as an instrument of bondage to sin, from which the "law of the Spirit of life" has set us free (Romans 7:23-25; 8:2; Galatians 3:23; 5:1).

This law that gives freedom, however, is parallel to the word of God (James 1:22-23). This is the word by which we received the new birth (James 1:18) which is able to ensure our salvation (James 1:21) and which has been implanted in our hearts (James 1:21). So, the law that gives freedom is the word, or teaching of Christ, that includes his commands and promises (Galatians 6:2; 2 Peter 3:2).

Why does the law give us freedom? The law gives freedom because it is obedience that results in doing God's law. That is when true freedom is found. If we simply listen to and yield to our emotions and give in to all our desires, we are enslaved. But when we accept God's will and obey it, we are truly free to be what God created us to be.

As followers of Christ, we obey not because we have to but because we want to! Obedience is never coerced. Obedience is freedom. We are free to obey. God's word, the law of freedom, has set us free – free from the power of sin and free from condemnation. Jesus taught us that knowing and obeying his teachings brings freedom (John 8:31-32).

And it is a perfect law of freedom. Why is that? James calls it the royal law (James 2:8). Why the royal law? It is the foundational principle that Jesus spelled out for us: "You must love the Lord your God with all your heart, with all your being, and with all your mind. This is the first and greatest commandment. And the second is like it: You must love your neighbor as you love yourself. All the Law and the Prophets depend on these two commandments" (Matthew 22:37-40).

Do you know what the perfect law calls us to do as Christ followers? It calls us to love God unconditionally and unapologetically and to love others as we love ourselves. As believers, we are free to live as God created us to live – loving God and loving others.

In the end, we remember that God's word in us is like a seed that is planted that helps us grow in salvation. It is like a mirror that clearly reflects the condition of the one looking into it. And it is like a law that provides freedom to be who we really are in Christ.

James leaves no stone unturned. As we shall discover, he has something also to say about the use of the tongue (3:1-12). And he has something to say about the treatment of the marginalized and those in need.

When we love God and love others it should be put into practice in our speech and actions. The way that others will know whether or not our faith is real is by the way we speak and what we choose to talk about.

James raises the stakes for us as followers of Christ. If we fail to keep a tight rein on our tongue, then what we profess (our religion) is not worth much and we are guilty of self-deception. Failing to control the tongue not only indicates a lack of wisdom and maturity, but also calls into question the validity of our profession of faith. Such a person is deceived (James 1:22) and his or her religion has no value whatsoever. Verbal actions speak louder than religious rituals.

And then James explains religion in terms of practical service and personal purity and piety. True religion consists not merely in holding to a correct set of doctrines, but also living in harmony with those doctrines. Again, walk the talk. Live and walk the faith 24/7.

How should our Christian *conduct* look? By caring for the helpless and defenseless. This is a theme that is prevalent throughout the Old Testament with references to orphans and widows. Micah 6:8 says, "He has told you, what is good and what the LORD requires from you: to do justice, embrace faithful love, and walk humbly with your God." By caring for the powerless and defenseless people, we most visibly put God's word into practice.

How should our Christian *character* look? By keeping ourselves from being polluted by the world. And how do we do that? By committing ourselves to live out Christ's ethical, radical and moral teachings, not the world's.

A true response to God's Word is both outward activity and inward control. I like what William Barclay concludes, "All through history, people have tried to make ritual and liturgy a substitute for sacrifice and service. They have made religion splendid *within* the church at the expense of neglecting it *outside* the church. This is by no means to say that it is wrong to seek to offer the noblest and the most splendid worship within God's house, but it is to say that all such worship is empty and idle unless it sends people out to love God by loving one another and to walk more purely in the tempting ways of the world."

It all comes down to walking the talk and living the Christian life 24/7. There is no break or time off in living the Christian life.

Words to Live by from the Church Fathers

OECUMENIUS: *When James says "quick to hear" he is not talking about simple listening but about eagerness to put into practice what has been heard. For he distinguishes quite clearly between the person who is ready to act on what he has heard and the one who is weighed down by laziness and procrastination, sometimes even to the point of never attempting to do anything at all.*

ANDREAS: *If we do not remember what we have seen and apply it in our deeds, then we shall lose the grace which has been given to us. But the one who remembers that he has been born again from on high, that he has been justified, and sanctified and counted among the children of God, will not give himself over to works which reject that grace.*

BEDE: *Spiritual happiness is gained not by empty words but by putting our good intentions into practice.*

AUGUSTINE: *Truth is more safely heard than preached. For when it is heard, lowliness is preserved, but when it is preached some bit of boastfulness may steal in almost unawares, and this brings corruption.*

BEDE (on quick to hear but slow to speak): *James is right to say this, for it is stupid to think that someone who is not prepared to learn from others will somehow be well equipped to preach to them. Someone who wants to become wise must first of all ask for this gift from God, as James has already said. Then he must find himself a good teacher and in the meantime discipline his tongue so that he says nothing useless but restricts himself to preaching the truth which he has recently learned from others.*

5

FAITH WITHOUT WORKS STINKS
James 2:14-26

"As the lifeless body is dead, so faith without actions is dead."
(James 2:26)

A young boy, on an errand for his mother, had just bought a dozen eggs. Walking out of the store, he tripped and dropped the sack. All the eggs broke and the sidewalk was a mess. The boy tried not to cry. A few people gathered to see if he was alright and to tell him how sorry they were. In the midst of the works of pity, one man handed the boy a quarter. Then he turned to the group and said, "I care 25 cents worth. How much do the rest of you care?"

Words do not mean much if we have the ability to do more. If we fail to put action and words together then nothing much will happen. That brings us to this big subject of faith and works as it relates to 24/7 living.

If you want to talk some theology, James gives us the most theologically significant and perhaps the most controversial part of his letter when he talks about the contrast between faith and works in 24/7 living.

While discussing those New Testament writings he regarded as central to the gospel, the fifteenth century church reformer and monk Martin Luther dismissed the Letter of James as "an epistle of straw." His reason for this reference was that he believed it had little doctrinal value as compared to other books in the New Testament, not because he questioned whether it should be a New Testament book and included in the Bible. He mistakenly read James as advocating a view of faith and works which contradicts that of the rest of scripture, especially in the way Paul addressed it in his New Testament letters.

However, for John Wesley, the founder of Methodism, this small letter was central for Christian faith and life. In his journal, he described James as a remedy against the general temptation of leaving off good works in order to increase faith. Elsewhere, in his Sermon 61 on "The Mystery of Iniquity" he observed that, when James wrote his letter, "That grand pest of Christianity, a faith without works, was spread far and wide; filling the Church with a 'wisdom from beneath,' which was 'earthly, sensual, devilish,' and which gave rise, not only to rash judging and evil speaking, but to 'envy, strife, confusion, and every evil work'".

Faith and works. It is an important contrast to think about in our lives. The big question we should be concerned with, as was James, is whether authentic faith can be separated from a life of obedience to God. Is it possible for us to have experienced the new birth, repented of our sins, and embraced Christ as Savior, and yet continue to live just as before, with no essential change in conduct, speech, attitudes, motives, and desires? Is it possible to possess a genuine faith which exerts no transformative influence on our behavior?

The answer from James is a resounding "No!" Such a separation between faith and works is contrary to the very nature of a living, saving faith and therefore cannot exist. It is a purely imaginary concept.

Let us be clear about one thing right from the start. James does not argue that works must be *added* to faith in order to accomplish salvation. Nor does he argue that works *in and of themselves* have saving power. Instead, we are reminded of the powerful truth that works are the necessary and inevitable consequence of a faith that goes beyond mere intellectual assent. A tree's visible fruit testifies to the life within it. So it is in our lives. The fruit of our lives is to gives witness to the life of the Holy Spirit that is within us.

A profession of faith in Christ is just that – a profession. It must be examined. It must be looked at. It must be evident.

Works, as James chooses to define the term, refers to actions taken in obedience to God's word.

The Christian life is not about the relative quantity or quality of our works. It is not about a life that professes the faith but gives no evidence whatsoever of regeneration.

Can a kind of faith - one which does not produce works - save us? Asking that question anticipates a negative answer. I have heard some argue, in an attempt to safeguard the doctrine of salvation by faith, that James' use of the word "save" refers only to escaping some earthly peril. But in the context of James, it is clearly the eternal salvation of our souls which is in view (James 1:21; 4:12; 5:20).

To prove a point, James earlier gave us a one-line example of the kind of works that gives evidence of genuine faith: caring for the basic physical needs of other believers who are in poverty (James 1:27). He likely has in mind the teaching of Jesus that failing to show acts of mercy and compassion reveals a kind of self-condemning lack of love, not only for the poor, but for Christ himself (Matthew 25:41-46).

Here is the point being made by James in this example. It is the uselessness and hypocrisy of offering mere words of comfort when what is actually needed is to take action to relieve suffering. Inaction belies words and calls into question sincerity. Does a person who wishes others well while refusing to lift a hand to help them genuinely care for their welfare? Absolutely not. Pious words not only are ineffectual, they are false.

Think of it this way. If you tell someone you will pray for them in a time of need and fail to do it, it becomes just a simple pious expression or a matter of habit. It is the nice and right thing for a Christian to say. But it is detached from any action. Pious words that do not result in action just represent our desire to think of ourselves as a caring or spiritual person, or perhaps just an attempt to induce the poor or needy person to move along or get out of our way. Then their inconvenient need can be put out of sight and out of mind. But of all the things such empty words could represent, true love and concern are not on the list of possibilities.

The fact is that any so-called faith which does not produce the fruit of active obedience to God is likewise dead. It is barren and dead in both an external and internal sense. Not only does it produce no benefit to anyone, but it fails to do so because it is without life. It is inherently defective. So, it lacks authenticity and is false.

The challenge that James gives us is simple: Can you prove the validity of your faith – without works? No. But you and I can demonstrate our faith *through* our works.

It is a false faith that produces no works at all. But there is also another kind of so-called faith that is just mere intellectual assent or agreement with a set of theological teachings or propositions.

James makes clear that even the demons believe what is fundamentally true about God - that there are not many gods, but only one (Deuteronomy 6:4). And yet it does them no good just to believe and profess. They are still condemned to eternal torment and they tremble in fear at that knowledge (Matthew 8:29). Likewise, for someone to recite and believe the Apostle's Creed, the Nicene Creed, the Westminster Confession of Faith, or any other statement of doctrine or faith, is not in itself sufficient for saving faith. It takes more than a creed and a confession of faith. Anyone can recite a creed.

A person who continues to maintain the validity of faith-without-works is not only empty-headed, but empty in a spiritual sense – they lack true saving faith. Faith without works is a faith that does not work. It is simply useless.

Do you remember the story of Abraham, the patriarch of the Old Testament? For Jewish Christians in the Early Church, there could be no more powerful example than that of Abraham. Not only was he the physical progenitor of the Jewish race, but he is also the spiritual father of all, both Jew and Gentile, who share in his faith (Romans 4:11-17). We know that Abraham was revered by Jews as a man of great righteousness. His obedience when commanded to offer Isaac as a sacrificial offering (Genesis 22) was viewed as the supreme example of his faithfulness to God.

The apostle Paul said that it was Abraham's faith, rather than his works, which was "credited to him as righteousness" (Galatians 3:6; see Romans 3:28; 4:1-9). Don't be confused. It is not a contradiction with James. Paul and James use the terms "faith," "works" and "justify" in different ways and for different purposes.

Let us think about Paul first. For Paul, the justification (righteousness or salvation) in view is primarily legal or forensic. He is concerned with the question of how a sinful person can stand before the judgment seat of God and receive a verdict of not guilty. The works which he rejects as having no saving value are works of the law. These are acts done in compliance with the Torah in order to merit God's favor. And the faith which he views as the sole grounds for God's pronouncement of being righteous is a genuine faith. It is a faith that involves repentance from sin and embracing Christ in his words and his works.

For James, however, the question is different. What constitutes genuine faith? His answer is that a faith which produces no works or that consists only of cognitive assent is not really faith at all. The works he has in mind do not earn salvation for us but rather confirm the authenticity of our faith. Therefore, to be pronounced righteous, or justified, on the basis of these works is not to assert that they have saving value in and of themselves. It is to understand them as a clear demonstration that validates our saving faith which produces them! It is a faith that works!

Abraham was considered righteous, or justified, not on the basis of his offering of Isaac in itself, but on the basis of his faith (Genesis 15:6), a faith to which that act of sacrifice gave irrefutable proof. His faith was confirmed, and thus he was vindicated as righteous, by this "work" (Hebrews 11:17-19).

Did you get that? Abraham's faith and the actions which revealed it were not in opposition but cooperated with one another. This is not *synergism*, in which faith and works both are viewed as contributing to salvation; rather, works are the natural expression and fulfillment of saving faith. So, the faith of Abraham, on the basis of which he was graciously declared righteous (Genesis 15:6; Rom. 4:3-5), was confirmed by and through the offering of Isaac which brought that faith to fruition and on full display (see Genesis 22:12).

This is true for the simple reason that the "faith alone" to which James refers (faith which stands by itself with no accompanying works) is not true faith at all, but an impostor. As the Reformation slogan puts it, "Faith alone saves, but the faith that saves is not alone".

This is about those in the church who make a profession of faith but show little, if any, evidence of actually following Jesus. The matter is framed clearly for all who profess Christ. When a Christian sees someone in desperate need and does nothing about that need except to pronounce a flippant and trite greeting, then what good does that do? This is but another way of asking if a person who ignores the suffering of sisters and brothers in Christ has a genuine (justifying) faith in Christ.

The stark reality is that faith by itself, if it does not have works, is dead.

The ethic in all of this is that someone who will not help a brother or sister in a time of crisis is acting in such a way that we may question whether or not they have ever exercised saving faith in the first place. Those are strong words for sure.

No doubt about it, a profession of faith without any accompanying works is not a credible profession. A true faith is not a *stand-alone* kind of faith. A true faith is accompanied by good works. In fact, a true faith (and trust) in Christ produces good works. This is why James can be so emphatic about the fact that someone who claims to have faith but lets his brother and sister go unclothed and hungry may not have true faith.

Let us sharpen the point a bit more. In James 2:18, he speaks of the objection raised by a hypothetical questioner who does not see any necessary connection between the presence of faith in Christ and the presence of good works. We simply cannot allow for the possibility that someone can have a truth faith without works, or (on the flip-side) that there can be someone who has genuine good works which do not spring from faith.

Faith and works are like Siamese twins. They are inseparable and the relationship between them is crystal clear. A genuine faith is the cause of good works (the effect). And works done apart from faith are not really good. The presence of good works is the sign that faith is authentic and living.

Be reminded that in James 2 we are told even a demon believes that there is one God! That is, demons assent to the truth of the proposition that there is one God who will certainly punish them eternally on the last day causing them to shudder. What is the difference between what demons believe about God and what some professing Christian believes if that so-called faith never leads to the outward evidence of good works?

Christians may give assent to the truth – they believe every article of the Creed to be true – but they never truly trust Christ. They never allow what is in their heads to make its way into their hearts and then find expression in their lives. Someone can believe the right things about God and yet not have genuine saving faith. The standard which James applies throughout this epistle to tell which is which (which is genuine saving faith and which is a *mere profession* of faith) is the presence of good works. As James sees it, if faith is genuine, good works will be present.

Let us get it right. If we say that we belong to Christ, true faith will not discriminate against the poor, favor the rich, nor ignore the naked and hungry. Faith and works has to do with compassion.

It really is quite simple. The Bible never tells us to go to a church building each week, sing three hymns, take an offering, and then listen to a sermon. Nowhere is church going presented as a way to discharge our obligation to God. Genuine faith and worship of God flows out of our love for God. This love, however, is meant to drive us outward in acts of compassion. We should never be seen passing by an opportunity to act compassionately.

We must love God. This is the vertical relationship of our faith. We must love others. This is the horizontal relationship of our faith. Both of these elements must always be on our hearts. Loving those we see in church each week helps us to grow as disciples of Christ. Christianity is intensely congregational. The religion of the Bible is all about relating to each other in tight-knit fellowships.

That said, the purpose of our discipleship (following Christ) is to transform the world. We cannot do what Jesus calls us to do and be shy, racist, bigoted, or *holier than thou*. We must be compassionate toward strangers, to the marginalized, the needy, the poor, the powerless and defenseless. None of us are free to be one-hour-a-week Christians. Every gift that God has given us must be shared.

Too often the central problem with us as Christians has been described so vividly by Peter Marshall: "Church members in too many cases are like deep sea divers, encased in suits designed for many fathoms deep, marching bravely to pull out plugs in bathtubs."

It is a sad and true reality that week-by-week too many churches in the United States are getting smaller and becoming more trivial. The heyday of full pews and bursting Sunday school classrooms is now 60 years back in the rear view mirror. The cause of this is not lack of resources, nor has the Holy Spirit stopped teaching Christians how to live their faith.

We are well equipped in every way, but it is quite apparent that we would rather be a polite weekly gathering of friends than an intense, caring, fellowship. It seems that we would rather fix the stuck bathtub stoppers of our church buildings than be at work, living out our faith, and faithfully seeking to transform the world we are called to serve with compassion, love, and grace-filled works.

Our faith should work along with our works. When our faith works in this way then our faith is authentic. It is real. It is validated.

Think about it again. It really is a matter of perspective. It really makes sense. How are people justified? – by faith alone. How do we tell if faith is genuine? – our faith is justified by works.

Just as a corpse can do nothing when the spirit departs, so too someone who claims to have faith but who does not have works has dead faith (and is therefore not alive).

If God has brought us forth through the word, we have a living faith and we are justified before God apart from works. But if we have a living faith – given to us to us by God – we will also do good works, proving that our faith is genuine.

Here is the way it works. If our faith is genuine, when the need arises we will care for the poor, clothe the naked, and feed the hungry. If our faith is genuine, we will strip off our sins just as we would take off our dirty clothes. If our faith is genuine, we will not discriminate against the poor or show favoritism to the rich. If our faith is genuine, we will tame our tongues and not seek to be friends with the world. If our faith is genuine, we will not boast about tomorrow and we will be patient in our suffering.

Because Jesus Christ has died for our sins (our infractions of the law) and because he has perfectly obeyed God's commandments (fulfilling all righteousness), we are justified through our faith in Christ. But that faith in Christ is proved genuine when good works flow out of justifying faith. That is how we know that "faith apart from works is dead."

The fact is neither faith nor works can be cut off and thrown away like a straw. The reality is that if you have faith then works will naturally be a product. You cannot get rid of works just because they do not save you. You cannot sever the effect from the cause. Just as an apple tree will bear apples, so faith will produce good works.

Faith and works are not enemies. True faith and righteous works go hand in hand. They are two parts of God's work in us. Faith brings a person to salvation and works bring that person to faithfulness. Faith is the cause and works are the effect.

Pious clichés and Christian verbiage are not the evidence of saving faith. There must be a vocation to go along with the vocabulary. It must be lived 24/7 as we walk the talk.

Words to Live by from the Church Fathers

VALERIAN OF CIMIEZ: *What does it profit to bewail another man's shipwreck if you take not care of his body, which is suffering from exposure? What good does it do to torture your soul with grief over another's wounds if you refuse him a health-giving cup?*

LEO THE GREAT: *While faith provides the basis for works, the strength of faith comes out only in works.*

ANDREAS: *If someone does not show by his deeds that he believes in God, his profession of faith is worthless. For it is not the one who just says that he is the Lord's who is a believer, but the one who loves the Lord so much that he is prepared to risk even death because of his faith in him.*

6

THAT LITTLE BIG THING
CALLED THE TONGUE
James 3:1-12

"In the same way, even though the tongue is a small part of the body, it boasts wildly." (James 3:5)

On a windswept hill in an English country churchyard stands a drab, gray slate tombstone. The faint etchings read:

Beneath this stone, a lump of clay, lies Arabella Young, Who, on the twenty-fourth of May, began to hold her tongue.

Let us hope that we learn what that woman never did, to tame the tongue! As a wise sage observed, "As you go through life you are going to have many opportunities to keep your mouth shut. Take advantage of all of them."

I remember reading that "words are also works." Given all that we understand about the Book of James so far, it should come as no surprise that at some point in this letter James would tackle the subject of our speech to one another. In so doing, James has some powerful words of caution on how destructive our words can be and why we struggle to tame our tongue.

If you know anything about Southern California, you are all too familiar with frightening scenes of wind-driven brush fires consuming everything in their path. When a brush fire strikes, vital watershed, expensive properties and homes are destroyed in minutes. People and animals are displaced, the skies turn black, and panic is the rule of the day.

When it comes to the tongue, James reminds us that a more powerful kind of damage can be done almost instantaneously by the human tongue. The words which we speak are capable of great destruction. Just as a small spark can create a horrific fire, our words can inflict great personal pain, or even destroy someone's reputation they have worked a lifetime to build.

And it is even more striking that our words may well reveal how deeply and thoroughly sin resides in our hearts. The words which we speak reveal to everyone our deepest thoughts. They reveal our true character. They expose how wise we may or may not be. A brush fire causes great havoc and damage. But the damage done by a fire often pales in comparison to the damage which can be done by the human tongue.

You probably are thinking right now that when James starts talking about the tongue, he has gone from preaching to meddling! He has just made it clear that genuine faith *works*. If God has changed your heart through the new birth, the saving faith that He granted you will inevitably show itself in a life of good deeds.

But now he moves from the *generality* of good deeds to the *specifics* of the words you speak. Genuine faith yields to Christ's lordship over the tongue. While the little big thing called the tongue may never be totally tamed, if you know Christ as Savior you are engaged in the ongoing battle to tame the terrible tongue.

It is a difficult but true admission that the tongue is one of the major battlegrounds we engage in 24/7 living.

It seems to me that James is a savvy pastor-teacher who knows that we will not gear up for the battle and face the sins of the tongue unless we recognize the magnitude of the problem. We all find a way, too easily, to justify ourselves by pointing to others who are notoriously bad. In comparison with how they talk, I am doing okay – so we say! Plainly said, the nature of our speech must reflect our profession of faith in Christ.

Before tackling the destructive nature of the tongue in James 3:1-12, James gives us a reminder that we will be held accountable for what we say.

He does this around the role of being a teacher. Simply stated, he warns teachers (of the word) that any who presume to teach the word will be judged by God with a greater strictness.

In James' day, a teacher would be someone like a Rabbi who was charged with the task of teaching from the Scriptures – in this case, the Old Testament.

So, anyone who presumes to teach should be fully aware that they will be held to a higher standard than those who are being taught. Why is this? Because the responsibility to teach correctly is great. And to teach incorrectly about the gospel has such serious consequences upon the hearers – leading people astray from the truth and to a false confidence in human righteousness.

One way to tame the tongue is to recognize that we all will be held accountable for our speech. Jesus said, "I tell you that people will have to answer on Judgment Day for every useless word they speak. By your words you will be either judged innocent or condemned as guilty" (Matthew 12:36-37). Jesus was not teaching justification by works. Rather, like James, Jesus was teaching that our works reveal whether our faith is genuine faith. Our words either validate that we are true believers or reveal that we do not know God. If we sin with our speech, we need to ask God's forgiveness and also the forgiveness of the one we sinned against. Genuine believers have this sense of being accountable for their speech.

When James talks about the tongue he uses some vivid illustrations to help us get a grip on how serious the problem of the tongue really is. He does this to prove the power of the tongue and how such a seemingly insignificant body part can exercise so much destructive power.

James uses two analogies to make the point that the tongue is small, but mighty: the bit and the rudder. A bit is a relatively small instrument, but when you put it into a horse's mouth you can control the entire horse. The same thing is true of a ship's rudder. It is relatively small compared to the size of the ship, but with his hand on the wheel or tiller the pilot can steer a mammoth ship, even in a strong wind.

James' point of comparison is not so much the matter of control (the tongue does not really control the body), but of the inordinate influence of such a small part: "In the same way, even though the tongue is a small part of the body, it boasts wildly" (James 3:5). Do not underestimate the power of the tongue, because if you do, you will not be able to tame it. There may be a comparison in the sense of influencing direction. If you control your tongue, it can direct your whole life into what is acceptable in God's sight. If you do not control your tongue, it will get you into great trouble!

Both the bit and the rudder must overcome contrary forces to direct the horse and the ship. A horse is a powerful animal that can do much useful work, but only if it can be directed. A ship is a useful means of transporting cargo or people, but if the rudder is broken it will be at the mercy of the wind and waves and could result in a shipwreck causing the loss of life and cargo. To work properly and accomplish good things, both bit and rudder must be under the control of a strong hand that knows how to use them properly. In the same way, the tongue must overcome the contrary force of the flesh and be under God's wise control if it is to accomplish anything good.

I remember growing up as child in Wichita, Kansas, where my father pastored. Behind the parsonage was a rather wide alley. That is where all the neighborhood children gathered to play, likely because it got us away from the busy residential streets. But it was also a place where it was easy to get into arguments and have a bit of neighborhood bully rivalry, if you will. I remember a neighborhood bully by the name of Charlie. He was often prone to foul language and name calling. For whatever reason, Charlie liked to pick on me – likely because I was a bit shorter and smaller than he was at the time. I think he also somehow knew that my parents forbid me to use foul language and resort to name calling! Since he resorted often to name calling, in order to protect myself and appear strong, I was known to repeat more than once these words: "Sticks and stones may break my bones, but words will never hurt me."

I believe James would vigorously disagree with that familiar children's taunt. The Book of James is steeped in the Old Testament, and it (especially the Book of Proverbs) has much to say about the power of the tongue, either for good or for evil. Proverbs 12:18 states, "Some chatter on like a stabbing sword, but a wise tongue heals." Just imagine that everyone who came to your church for worship were carrying into church an unsheathed, razor-sharp, two-edged sword. It would be a miracle if you got through the morning without anyone getting cut! The fact is, we all have a razor-sharp, two-edged sword - in our mouths! We should use our tongues and the words we speak with the greatest care to bring healing and grace, not hate and injury.

Proverbs 16:24 states, "Pleasant words are flowing honey, sweet to the taste and healing to the bones." If we all would read Proverbs frequently and pay attention to its wisdom, we would be a source of sweetness and healing in our homes, in our churches, and in our culture!

Even while writing this book, I noted that several Christian friends of mine were attacked and lied about on social media – by other Christians! While I do not recall having been lied about on social media, I am aware that I have been lied about in other ways. I know how it feels to have words like stabbing swords spoken or written to me. Those of us who name ourselves as Christ-followers should be better than this! Whatever happened to loving and encouraging one another? To our own detriment and destruction, we have too easily forgotten the simple command, "Instead, encourage each other, especially as you see the day drawing near" (Hebrews 11:25). It is high time we quit destroying each other with the various forms of social media we have at our disposal. When used in this way, it becomes nothing more than a gossip destructive tool of Satan. We should all be reminded that we are forgiven sinners, redeemed by God's grace. We must seek to be encouragers, not destroyers. Our words should bring healing, not harm.

There are two more word pictures used in James 3 for comparison and contrast: a forest fire and tamed animals. In my first pastoral assignment I lived in Washington State in the beautiful Northwest. I lived among some of the most beautiful evergreen forests anywhere in the United States. But everyone who lived in that area was very much aware of the potential danger and damage of forest fires. If you traveled into the forest areas, there were plenty of posted signs reminding us that fire is a great danger. The signs clearly posted to "put out the fires and don't leave them unattended." All it takes is one tossed cigarette or one campfire that is not totally extinguished and thousands of acres of beautiful forest can be destroyed. Under control, fire is useful; out of control, it is frightening and devastating!

I remember the news report in November of 1980 while I was living in the Northwest. After a very dry autumn, on an extremely windy day an arsonist lit a fire in the tinder-dry brush just above San Bernardino, California. The high winds quickly fanned the flames up the mountain toward the town of Crestline. While firefighters were trying to contain that blaze, the same arsonist drove to the east and then back to the west, lighting separate fires in each location. Many people who lived on the mountain had only a few hours notice to evacuate their homes for several days, so that they would not be trapped if the flames came up that far. Several homes in San Bernardino were destroyed, killing at least four people. Forest fires are devastating!

In James 3:6, there is a really direct statement. "The tongue is a small flame of fire, a world of evil at work in us. It contaminates our entire lives. Because of it, the circle of life is set on fire. The tongue itself is set on fire by the flames of hell." Scholars debate as to how to translate and punctuate this verse, but however it is done the point is clear. The tongue is a deadly, powerful source of evil that taints every part of our being. If we do not use our tongues with great caution, we are like spiritual arsonists, lighting careless fires that cause widespread destruction.

And if you are the one who is careless with the tongue, you are the first to be defiled. An unchecked tongue is the world of evil at work within us and contaminates our entire lives and hurts others as well.

Do you remember the earlier statement in James 1 where it says that true religion requires bridling the tongue and keeping oneself unstained by the world? Like a spark that lights a bigger fire, it not only defiles us but also sets on fire the course of our life. If you have a careless tongue it damages your entire life!

You may be wondering as I often have why it is that James uses such strong language to remind us that the tongue is set on fire by the flames of hell. On the surface, that expression seems more than overbearing. To be sure, those are really strong words that pack a wallop and leave us wondering.

A little bit of word meaning research reveals that the word used for *hell* is actually a transliteration of two Hebrew words meaning, "Valley of Hinnom." I have visited this valley, just outside the walls of Jerusalem, on my several trips to the land of Israel. This is the valley where the Jewish worshipers of Molech burned their children as sacrifices to appease the pagan idol by the same name. It later became a place to burn trash. The only other New Testament use is by Jesus (11 times) to refer to the place of eternal torment.

So, James clarifies with a vivid word picture that an evil tongue is set on fire by the evil one, Satan, himself! Those strong words should make us stop and shudder a bit.

All Christians would shrink back from sins like molesting children, satanic worship, or murder as being grossly depraved. There should be no doubt at all about these sins. Yet, how often do we tolerate gossip, slander, deceit, half-truths, sarcastic put-downs, and other sins of the tongue as if they were no big deal? James says that all such sins have their origin in the pit of hell. They defile the one committing them. They destroy others. As a believer in Christ, you must confront these sins in yourself and you must be bold and courageous enough to confront them in others.

James goes on to use an analogy from the animal world. If you have been to Sea World, you have seen trained whales, dolphins, and seals. At the circus, you have seen trained elephants, lions, and tigers. But James says that there is one beast that cannot be tamed: the human tongue! When untamed, the tongue "is a restless evil, full of deadly poison." Being restless means there is never a time when it sleeps. You must always be on guard against it. Being full of deadly poison, you should handle it as cautiously as you would a vial of anthrax.

James does *not* say that the tongue is untamable. He says that *no person* can tame it. It is *humanly* untamable. Only God can tame it. When the Holy Spirit controls your heart on a daily basis, over time the fruit of the Spirit will appear. These include love, patience, kindness, gentleness, and self-control, which all relate to the control of the tongue. To tame this terrible tongue, you must daily walk in the Spirit, taking every thought captive to the obedience of Christ. Ultimately, an evil tongue is the tool of an evil heart.

"Who are you," says James, "to judge another?" The sin of arrogant slander arrogates to oneself divine powers of knowing the hearts of others and being able to condemn them with our tongue. It operates so consistently that we may not even be aware of its nature, from the whispered remark behind the hand in the pew or at a board meeting, through the screaming tabloid headlines, to the gossip of television talk show hosts. The willingness to use speech to destroy others in order to realize a temporary sense of superiority has become a manifestation of arrogance so widespread it has become normalized in our culture. James reminds us that it is a form of speech that is "death-dealing poison" (3:8).

There is another problem that can come with the tongue. It has to do with a gross inconsistency that is too many times observed.

Christians say "Praise the Lord" in one breath and in the next breath they say evil or hurtful things about another person. They sit in church singing hymns to God and no sooner get out the door than they whisper, "Did you see so-

and-so? She makes me sick! She's such a hypocrite. Why, do you know what she did?"

This is something that ought not to be among those who profess the name of Christ. When this happens it is contrary to all of nature. The same spring does not send out fresh water one minute and bitter water the next. A fig tree does not produce olives. A vine does not produce figs. Salt water cannot produce fresh water.

What is the point? Jesus said, "Children of snakes! How can you speak good things while you are evil? What fills the heart comes out of the mouth" (Matthew 12:34). Or consider these words of Jesus, "But what goes out of the mouth comes from the heart. And that's what contaminates a person in God's sight" (Matthew 15:18). The mouth is simply the opening that vents whatever is in the heart. If there is raw sewage in the heart, there will be raw sewage gushing from the mouth! That is why Proverbs 4:24 reminds us, "More than anything you guard, protect your mind, for life flows from it."

Have you ever thought about how terribly embarrassing life would be if there were a direct open line between your thoughts and your mouth so that you blurted out loud whatever you were thinking? Instead of your polite, "I'm pleased to meet you," out comes, "I couldn't care less about meeting you!" After listening to someone drone on about something, instead of, "Yes, that's very interesting," you blurt out, "How can I get away from this bore?"

This is not to suggest that we should abandon politeness and become brutally blunt. But it is to say that even if you control your tongue, you still may well have a heart problem, too. If you want to tame the terrible tongue the place to start is with your heart.

Work daily at taking every thought captive to the obedience of Christ (2 Corinthians 10:5). Walk daily under the control of the Holy Spirit (Galatians 5:18). Renew your mind by memorizing Scripture (Romans 12:1-2; Psalm 119:11)

In all matters of the tongue and the way we practice 24/7 habits of speech, we can always make good on Ephesians 4:29: "Don't let any foul words come out of your mouth. Only say what is helpful when it is needed for building up the community so that it benefits those who hear what you say."

There is a Jewish Rabbi by the name of Joseph Telushkin. He has lectured around the country on the powerful and often negative impact of words. He has asked audiences if they can go for twenty-four hours without saying any unkind words about, or to, anybody. He says, "Invariably, a minority of listeners raise their hands signifying 'yes,' some laugh, and quite a large number call out, 'no!'"

He responds, "Those who can't answer 'yes' must recognize that you have a serious problem. If you cannot go for twenty-four hours without drinking liquor, you are addicted to alcohol. If you cannot go for twenty-four hours without smoking, you are addicted to nicotine. Similarly, if you cannot go for twenty-four hours without saying unkind words about others, then you have lost control over your tongue." He goes on to say, "There is no area of life in which so many of us systematically violate the Golden Rule."

So, what does Rabbi Telushkin do? He encourages his audiences to monitor their conversations for two days. "Note on a piece of paper every time you say something negative about someone who is not present. Also record when others do so, as well as your reactions when that happens. Do you try to silence the speaker, or do you ask for more details?" He adds, "To ensure the test's accuracy, make no effort to change the content of your conversations throughout the two-day period, and do not try to be kinder than usual in assessing another's character and actions." He states, "Most of us who take this test are unpleasantly surprised."

After all this, maybe you are wondering right now why it is that this little "common sense" Book of James fails to give us a list of helpful tips on how to control our tongue. Maybe it is because most of us, like the alcoholic, are in denial about the magnitude of the problem. The first step to dealing with the problem is to acknowledge, "I have a serious problem! I have a tool of the evil one in my own mouth!"

I like to think that James 3 could well be the key to the solution to so many of the ills in church, home, and societal life today. It is forest fire season. Things are tinder dry in our nation, churches, schools, culture, homes, and in our relationships. You have a fire set among your members! Do not add to the fire. Help put out the fire. Ask God often to tame your tongue! Live in control of your tongue 24/7! Only then can you walk your talk.

Words to Live by from the Church Fathers

CYRIL OF ALEXANDERIA: *The effective proof of a sound mind and perfect thought is to have nothing faulty on our tongue and to keep our mouths closed when necessary. For it is better to be guided by worthy speech, which is able to know and to express the fullness of all praise. For the most useful talent is to be able to speak wisdom when talking about how to live well. Foolish talk should be foreign to the saints.*

DIDYMUS THE BLIND: *In attacking what they say, James singles out the tongue, which is the instrument of speech. But since their thought are present in the body as a whole, it ought to be understood that his remarks apply to the entire body.*

BEDE: *The tongue is a fire which can destroy a whole forest of good works just by saying things which are evil. This fire is the exact opposite of that saving fire which is also like a tongue and which consumes all the dross and chaff of our vices, revealing the secrets of the heart. The saints are inflamed by it, they burn with love because of it, and by their preaching they set others ablaze like tongues of fire.*

CHRYSOSTOM: *Therefore, guard the tip of the tongue, for it is like a majestic stallion. For if you put a bit in its mouth and teach it to walk in order, it adapts to this and is satisfied. But if you let it run wild, it becomes the vehicle of the devil and his angels.*

7

THE PREJUDICE, POVERTY AND WEALTH THING
James 1:9-11; 2:1-13; 4:13-5:6

"It is a sin when someone knows the right thing to do and doesn't do it." (James 4:17)

The year was 1979. I was a 21-year-old Bible college student studying for pastoral ministry. My pastor father invited me to travel with him to Haiti to preach and help train pastors. Haiti was then and is now considered the poorest country in the Western Hemisphere. My honest admission is I had never, up to that time, been exposed to much material poverty, though I believe I had seen poverty expressed as having far less than I had growing up in my family.

One day my father and I, along with the resident missionary, were walking along a rowdy and busy street in the capital city of Port-au-Prince. I remember the evidence and faces of what I perceived then as mind-boggling and abject poverty beyond belief. I was in a culture I did not know. It was everywhere evident. I could hardly take two steps each time without someone approaching me from the front or behind for just a "penny or a quarter" to share with them. It was quite obvious they had little or nothing. I knew I did not have enough to give away for all the needs I saw around me.

My sense of being overwhelmed reached its zenith point when I felt a hand on my lower leg from behind. I stopped to turn around and there below me I noticed a man crawl-walking on all fours with rubber tire improvised pads on each limb seeking to soften his "walk." All he wanted from me was a bit of money to help him – maybe to make his life just a bit better than what it was at the moment. While I could not understand the words he spoke, his eyes and face spoke more clearly than any words could have. Yes, I felt uncomfortable because I was healthy and well and rich (by material standards) and he was in need and impoverished beyond belief. He wanted just a little bit from me to make it better for him.

Did you know that almost half the world – over three billion people – live on less than $2.50 per day? At least 80% of humanity lives on less than $10 a day. Seventy percent of those living on less than $2.50 per day are women. With global population expanding 80 million per year, former World Bank President James D. Wolfensohn cautioned that, unless we address "the challenge of inclusion," 30 years hence we will have 5 billion people living on less than two dollars per day.

Poverty. Wealth. Prejudice. When James talks about these subjects in this "gospel of common sense" as it relates to how we live the Christian life and interact with others in the world, he minces no words on these uncomfortable truths.

In the first-century world, society was dominated by social castes and wealthy land-owners. The first Christians lived in a world that was based on a system of honor and shame, a world not at all unlike our own today. Honor was given to those who were able to benefit you. Those who would try to disgrace you or bring your status down were to be shamed. It was all a status game just like we have today. Then, just as now, people were trying to get ahead of each other and value each other based on what someone else could or could not do for you.

As the divide between Judaism and Christianity began to grow, followers of Christ faced more and more persecution from the Jewish religious establishment. Many were cut off from all ties to family, work, and both the temple and the synagogue, because they became followers of Jesus. Evicted from the synagogue and rejected by their families, these followers of Christ then joined newly formed house-churches, but were being looked down upon in these assemblies because of their poverty, an important pastoral matter James addresses head-on.

It really should be no surprise in this "gospel of common sense" that James takes up a discussion of the evils of discrimination, favoritism, and partiality as it relates to prejudice as well as the wealthy and the poor.

Our materialistic culture is seducing Christians into an economic lifestyle that does not glorify God. The popularity of television programs such as "Lifestyles of the Rich and Famous" and the veneration of social groups such as the glamorous "yuppies" testify to our society's materialistic values, values that many Christians have adopted.

Even within the Christian community, believers are bombarded with unbiblical views of wealth. At one extreme are those who preach a prosperity gospel of "health and wealth" for all believers. At the other extreme are radical Christians who condemn all wealth and imply that *rich Christian* is a contradiction in terms.

That is why we need to listen to what James has to say. James is concerned about the class distinctions that arise among Christians within the faith community.

The word that James gives us about the issues of prejudice, poverty and wealth is direct and straight forward. It is a pretty clear-cut truth that we need to live out 24/7.

It is a simple instruction but hard truth. Show no partiality as you hold the faith (James 2:1). When we show favoritism or partiality we deny the faithfulness of our Lord Jesus Christ. As we shall discover, the practical point at hand is that we are not to judge people based upon their appearance – either their fine clothing or their disheveled appearance or low social standing.

In the community called out in Christ's name there is no place for class distinctions between the wealthy and the poor. And we are called to take notice of the typical games Christians can play when it comes to poverty, wealth and prejudice.

To help us understand a bit better, let us begin with a kind of paraphrase and put into perspective what James is talking about. In a contemporary 21st century it could read like this.

"If a person comes into your church with a gold ring and dressed in fine clothes, and there also comes in a poor person, say a homeless and unemployed person, in dirty and tattered clothes, looking disheveled, and no doubt, a bit smelly, and you pay special attention to the one who is wearing fine clothes, and say, 'You sit here in a good place up front,' so they can hear in a crowded place or sit by better ventilation, and you say to the poor person, 'You stand over there in the back,' where it is difficult to hear and oppressively warm, or 'You sit here at my feet,' a sign of very humiliating low-standing, then you have made distinctions among yourselves and become judges with evil motives."

This is a timeless illustration. James speaks as loudly today as when he penned the words. It is still not always easy to know how to accommodate a tramp in a worship service and it is still easy to assume that wealth gives a commanding voice in church affairs.

Many of us recognize ourselves or someone we know in this description. We are nervous if not irritated when, for example, a person – a stranger with seemingly bad habits and horrible odors – comes into our presence in the sanctuary. We may even surmise, "You do not belong here," even though we do not say it. And we may politely ask, "Are you lost?" as if to say, you should not be here!

The point is simply that Christians (those who have faith in the Lord Jesus Christ) act like non-Christians when they make rash distinctions about people solely on the basis of mere appearance.

To divide brothers and sisters in Christ on the basis of their social status and appearance is to place oneself in the position of a judge. To do it to anyone at all is even more judgmental. Such a right belongs to God alone. To do this is a manifestation of evil thoughts which Christians are supposed to be stripping off like dirty clothes.

When we show favoritism through prejudiced actions in any way, we act contrary to faith in the Lord of glory who has died for all his people (rich or poor) and who has called his people from all places and situations in life to faith in

Christ. To divide anyone on the basis of mere appearance is sinful.

Discrimination and partiality based upon mere appearance or economic status cannot be squared with the character of God. The fact is that God chooses to save both rich *and* poor. The irony in this is that it is God himself who chooses the poor and then makes them rich in faith.

If the poor trust Christ and love God it is not because they are poor but because they have been chosen by God with faith in Christ. By choosing both rich and poor and then forming them into one body (the Church) God is showing that he is actively undoing the effects of sin upon human society.

In choosing both rich and poor, God is doing what no sinful and broken human society can fully do in perfect ways – uniting different people from different races, cultures, and socio-economic backgrounds, into one body. Since God has chosen these poor among them to be rich in faith and to enter his kingdom, how can their fellow Christians discriminate against them because they are poor? To do so is sin, plain and simple.

Why is it wrong, then, to discriminate in favor of the wealthy and powerful? Simply because it contradicts God's own actions toward us.

Throughout redemptive history God has sought, not the high and mighty, but rather the lowly, the outcast, the least and the smallest to be the recipients of his grace (1 Corinthians 1:27-28). Love of the poor, downtrodden and helpless is written into the very heart and divine nature of God. It is written into the very fabric of who God is.

If we would follow Christ, then it must be our glory, as it was his, to be incessantly and preponderantly on the side of the poor, the underprivileged, the disadvantaged and the oppressed in our churches and in our society. There can be no excuses.

Jesus reminded us that it is difficult for those who are rich to enter the kingdom of God (Matthew 19:24). Why is that? Because they can too easily tend to be proud and self-sufficient rather than poor in spirit (Matthew 5:3), very simply, being humble and needy before God.

It is not simply for the sake of self-preservation that Christians must not practice favoritism, but because favoritism is a violation against God's intention toward us.

Over against the practice of favoritism, we have what we call the royal law of Scripture, "You shall love your neighbor as yourself" (Leviticus 19:18). It is called the royal law because Jesus uses it in the New Testament to summarize the law in regard to others.

Love of neighbor is the essence of Christian faith and obedience. We are to follow Jesus' example in loving our neighbors. We obey this commandment to love our neighbor by not discriminating or showing favoritism.

Would we want to be discriminated against or treated with contempt because of our economic status or any other reason? Of course not. Then neither should we treat others in this way.

Favoritism emulates, not the law of love, but the oppressive measures of the rich who do not show mercy. The polar opposite of favoritism is mercy.

This whole discussion about favoritism is provocative, because it seems to prohibit making any positive distinction whatsoever based on wealth. If something as relatively minor as offering reserved seating is condemned as evil (James 2:4) and as a violation of God's law (James 2:9), then what about other practices we get involved in as Christians?

The place where economic responsibility becomes most personal is in finances – how we gain and spend. Our Christian ethic is less interested in speculative theories of the economic order than in wisely using the resources we have been given and earned. We are given these resources by the Creator and we are called to improve them through our imagination, reason, and effort. It is not a side issue for Christians to deliberate personally how we gain and spend temporal resources. We must nurture habits of the practice of stewardship of God's gifts of time and possessions.

The poets of all ages have railed against money "as the grand corrupter of the world, the bane of virtue, the pest of human society." I would suggest rather than railing against money that we view it as a training ground for eternity. I believe that is what James seeks to teach us.

If James calls us to live out the life of Christ by caring for the poor, he is equally determined that we should not be dazzled by the rich. It is not all that long ago when the wealthy paid an annual rent to secure a well-placed seat in parish churches, while those who could not raise the financial wind had to be content with seats in the far-off corners bearing the actual label 'Free.'

Such blatant inequality is a thing of the past, as far as I know, but it is by no means unusual for a person to have a voice in church affairs related not to wisdom but to wealth – how much they have to give.

And it is all too common for well-heeled congregations to assume that they ought to have (and get) the most gifted pastors, while communities of faith in less promising or attractive areas cannot expect more than the so-called average – which is an inferior term in and of itself.

Would God consider it appropriate to name a building after a large donor? Ouch. I often wonder. Would God approve of populating church and ministry governing boards disproportionately with those who give significant sums? Ouch again. I have often wondered that as well.

Such actions are often justified by arguing that it is not the money itself which is being honored, but rather the donor's devotion to God as demonstrated by their financial sacrifice. However, too often such judgments about wealth and money simply reflect man's standard, not God's (see Mark 12:41-43; Luke 21:1-4).

It is a regretful reality that money still does the talking far too loudly in Christian circles and where and when it does it is a blight on those who profess the faith.

I remember some people in places where I have pastored who promised me that if I would just do "such-and such" when it came to mission and ministry then they would be willing to give the money to support it. The times when I was confronted by these kinds of people was often when there was some apparent conflicting situation in the life of the church and it came through loud and clear that if I would just "bend their way" they would throw their money at it. I have often remarked to people who confronted me in these situations, "If it is of God and for good, He will make it happen and He will provide. I will not have to be leveraged by money to see God do what He wants to do."

When we choose to abstain from showing partiality or making decisions based on wealth or outward appearance, we are only truly then identifying our real worth with Christ that is far greater than any earthly treasure. That is when we truly walk the talk of our faith. That is when we live out the truth 24/7.

We all have great riches in Christ (Ephesians 1:18). Giving special honor to those who possess worldly goods implies just the opposite; that what really matters are earthly riches. And when we make judgments based solely on externals, we are failing to reflect the character of our God who does not show favoritism (Ephesians 6:9). In short, we are not walking the talk. We are not living 24/7 the way God intends for us to live.

The point of this example in which a person of high economic status is given overtly preferential treatment over someone of low status is that any hierarchy of honor in the church that is based on worldly criteria is odious to God.

Regretfully, it is the nature of broken humanity to create such caste distinctions. Although James focuses on matters of economic disparity, it does not require a great interpretive leap to apply the principles to race, ethnicity, nationality and other such characteristics.

"Anyone who tries to keep all of the Law but fails at one point is guilty of failing to keep all of it" (James 2:10) This is one of the most powerful verses in the Bible to refute those who think that God will accept them because they are better than someone else.

The truth is that God does not grade on a curve. To violate any of his commands makes us just as guilty as if we had broken every one of them. We cannot pick and choose the ones we consider to be important or worth keeping. They all come from God and bear his authority. Therefore, to violate any command, no matter what the reason or excuse, is to disobey God himself.

The call to a higher standard of divine love, the kind of love God has for us, excels all other forms of love and is the distinctive call to Christian communities and disciples. This love is a radical call to unconditional justice wherever the economic gap between poverty and wealth is great.

How is that wealthy Christians seek to live lovingly and justly when brother and sister Christians live poor and destitute lives? The fact is that in an ideal world of Christian faith God's kind of love supersedes conditional love and partiality. But in our all too typical and limited world of everyday life, partiality and favoritism way too often appears to supersede God's kind of love.

This challenge by James is radical because it calls all Christians, rich and poor, to show no partiality.

We are reminded that we are called in every way "to speak and act as people who will be judged by the law of freedom" (James 2:12). We will be judged by the standards we practice (Matthew 7:1-2). And if we keep the whole law of love, but fail in one point – showing favoritism – the whole weight of the law falls upon us. And there is no mercy. No mercy? No mercy!

We are called to live and to walk the talk of a higher standard, the law of Jesus. This kind of faith is lived out in mercy toward others, especially the marginalized. And in the end, "mercy triumphs over judgment."

In the face of the "health and wealth" prosperity teaching that is screaming at us, sometimes literally, in our Christian culture, it needs to be known again that wealth and poverty are not the visible manifestation of God's ultimate blessing and curse. Wealth and poverty are part of God's mysterious providential purposes for his people. There will always be wealthy Christians and poor Christians, ideally becoming one people in Christ's church.

Wealth is not life's ultimate goal and poverty is not life's ultimate curse. Christians understand that while wealth and poverty are part of life, neither wealth nor poverty has anything to do with God's blessing poured out upon his people in Christ.

According to James, the poor, persecuted Jewish believer in Jesus had a wealth that those persecuting them could never understand. The wealthy Christian was called to understand that they have a great responsibility to be good stewards of their wealth. They must choose to identify with Christ in his suffering and with the suffering of his people, the poor and marginalized. A wealthy Christian knows that wealth can disappear in one blast of scorching heat (James 1:9-10). And yet, they too, like the poor Christian, possess a heavenly wealth that the twists and turns of this life can never take away.

To trust in wealth, power, and fame is to be contaminated by the world. Rather, both rich and poor are to boast in Christ because in Christ both are truly blessed beyond anything found in this life.

Actually, the poor and wealthy are called upon to find satisfaction in their status (James 1:9). But they do so in a way that is in direct opposition to the values of the world. The follower of Christ who lacks this world's goods and who is despised and looked down upon is encouraged not merely to persevere, but also to actually exult in his lofty status!

In truth, he or she is not poor, but rich, for they have been chosen by God to receive the crown of life and to inherit an eternal kingdom (James 1:12, 18; 2:5).

The pride which James endorses is not arrogance or self-centered boasting, but rather a kind of humility that looks to God as the source of one's true worth. The worth which the world assigns to people, based on temporary and external factors, is often completely off the mark.

We should not revel in thinking that we are somehow "masters of the universe" or "masters of our own fate." We are to see ourselves as those whose earthly life and riches are no more lasting than a flower wilting under the hot sun. Whether rich or poor, true worth and value come not from gold or silver but from our relationship with God through Jesus Christ.

What is offensive as ungodly and unspiritual is a self-sufficient attitude of envy and arrogance that leaves God out of the picture when looking to the future. It is an attitude that assumes we have the power to assure a positive outcome for our efforts or that we have both the ability and the right to shape events in any way we desire (James 4:13).

The brevity of human life and the need for wisdom to live well because of the brevity of life is abundantly clear in

Scripture. Life is like a breath (Psalm 39:5). Life is like grass which withers (Psalm 103:15-16). Life is like chaff which is scattered by the wind (Isaiah 40:23-24).

As Shakespeare's Macbeth laments:

"Out, out, brief candle!
Life's but a walking shadow, a poor player,
That struts and frets his hour upon the stage,
And then is heard no more."

There is a tendency for wealthy people to arrogantly suppose that they have full control and authority over their own lives. They often fail to recognize that God is sovereign over their plans and that they are accountable to Him.

When money is used for self-gratification within the temporary values of this world alone, it is rightly called, as John Wesley suggested, "the mammon of unrighteousness."

As William Ernest Henley wrote in "Invictus," they say to themselves, "*I am the master of my fate, I am the captain of my soul.*"

When we just view ourselves as being the masters of our own fate or the captain of our own souls then the requirements of a holy God become irrelevant. We become practical atheists. We believe in God but that belief makes no distinctive difference. Somehow we imagine that the strength of our own determination will allow us to prevail. How foolish! How tragically misguided! And yet, how seductive.

The sad reality is this has been the personal creed of countless people, both in James' day and ours. It seems attractive because it extols the virtues of courage and perseverance. But it fails to ground those qualities in a foundation of faith and submission to God. It falsely exalts man as supreme rather than his Creator. Although it may lead to worldly success, it will ultimately end in destruction.

It is so easy for us to associate *being* with *having*. Why is it that we always want to define who we are by what we have?

In our culture of commercialism and business conglomerates and multinational corporations, envy and arrogance rule. The bottom line of profit or loss is the only measure that gets considered. Success is measured by the amount of things (whatever they are) that can be accumulated.

And how about those of us who claim the name of Christ? How is our walk? Are there too many communities of faith that get co-opted by envy and arrogance? It may not be in monetary terms alone, but in membership and influence. When this happens, it is a deceptive way of wisdom that is from below and not above, earthbound and unspiritual.

It is not the mere fact of wealth that brings God's disfavor. It is the misuse and abuse of it. It is the unrighteous means by which it is obtained and sustained.

The wealthy are condemned because they hoard wealth, commit fraud by unjustly delaying payment or refusing payment for services rendered, withhold rightful pay from their workers, live in luxury and self-indulgence, and pervert the legal system to cause the death of the innocent (James 5:2-6). For a laborer who lives paycheck to paycheck or a small businessman who lives or dies by cash flow, such withholding represents a significant hardship.

James accuses the wealthy of using their money and influence to bias the legal system in their favor in order to deprive others of their property and thus their means of sustenance, in effect causing death by starvation. As is often the case, those who are unjustly treated do not have the means to adequately defend themselves and so cannot oppose them.

Many in our day would view these merely as sharp business practices perhaps used to extract concessions from one's labor force or suppliers. But James labels them clearly as sin.

James never says that God condemns wealth. God is the giver of wealth. What is condemned is wasteful self-indulgence. It is a condemnation when wealth is used for sinful pleasure and comfort. It is a condemnation when wealth is acquired through exploiting the back-breaking labor of migrant workers or refugees who are simply cheated out of their rightful and fair wages.

The writer Luke Timothy Johnson notes that being heedless of anything else but making a profit is one thing; committing actual violence against others in order to live luxurious on the earth is another and far more perverted form of arrogance.

Envy and arrogance can take and do take a public form in economic and political systems that privilege the few and punish the many, that exploit the resources of the earth for the extravagant life-style of those privileged to live in the first world rather than the third, that reduce the laborers in the fields (and factories and sweatshops and fast-food eateries) to slaves by systems of reward and taxation that perpetuate inequity, that so marginalize major portions of the population that they are unable to sustain their existence at a meaningful human level, that commit legal murder against the innocent by means of litigation and the corruption of the courts.

Here is the 24/7 reality for those who claim the name as Christ followers. We cannot close our eyes to these realities as followers of The Way. Even if we cannot by ourselves change them, somehow we must by our own lives challenge them. If we have envy and arrogance we stand within that same distorted view of the world and, therefore, under the same judgment of God.

It is true that not all rich people are evil or self-indulgent. But wealth has to be used ethically or else it will testify against us.

To put things in perspective, we often think of wealthy people in our American culture as having a huge house, nice vehicles, and at least $1 million+ in the bank. But by the world's standards even the poorest American is wealthy. If you have an internet connection in a place with electricity and you know how to read English, you are in the top 5% of the world's population when it comes to wealth.

So the call is not just on the few among us who have a tremendous amount of wealth relative to the rest of us. This call is to all of us to use what we have ethically, wisely, and in a way that pleases God.

James is not condemning wealth itself but the folly of trusting in that wealth which has been gained by exploiting others. As John Calvin so wisely puts it, "God has not appointed gold for rust, nor garments for moths; but on the contrary, he has designed them as aids and helps to human life."

The problem is not with wealth itself. Wealth is a gift from God. The problem is that we allow wealth and riches to become the *be all* and *end all* of life. What we forget is that riches will not last. Material possessions rot and decay. The finest clothes are eventually consumed by moths. Even precious metals eventually rust and tarnish.

James' warning about the dangers of wealth echoes the words of Jesus. Jesus warns us in Matthew 6:19-21, "Stop collecting treasures for your own benefit on earth, where moth and rust eat them and where thieves break in and steal them. Instead collect treasures for yourselves in heaven, where moth and rust don't eat them and where thieves don't break in and steal them. Where your treasure is, there your heart will be also."

Those who trust in their wealth – rather than the grace and mercy of God – will have their arrogance and unbelief exposed for all to see on the Day of Judgment. As Jesus points out, the rich who were exploiting the poor have allowed their trust and affections to be tied to their possessions. All the while their hearts have wandered far from the purposes and will of God. The same corrosion which exposes their folly will be used as evidence against them when all that they have accumulated is only so much evidence of their sinful arrogance.

Riches are a trap that many fall into and by which many are destroyed. Riches appear so attractive, dazzling the eyes. Yet they elicit hurtful inward desires that lead to destroyed lives both in this world and eternity. Regrettably very few resist these temptations. Even fewer take seriously the warnings to heart. Some who have been solemnly warned may quickly forget. And others who study the warnings of James may put a spin on it to make it seem of little consequence. But its consequences last from generation to generation.

It is the folly of that all too common sentiment expressed in the popular bumper sticker, "He who dies with the most toys wins."

Creatures such as we, whose lives are so vanishingly brief and who cannot ensure even our own moment-to-moment existence, should not live lives of blind, self-assuming confidence. Rather, we should always choose to acknowledge our dependence on God, in our speech, and more importantly, in our attitude and actions, always committing our plans to him. In fact, walk the talk. Live the life 24/7.

God is defender of the poor as well as the giver of wealth. There is great folly in storing up treasure on earth when we should be seeking that heavenly treasure which is found only in Christ.

The good news for all of us – whether we be rich, poor, or otherwise – is that in Christ we are given unspeakable wealth, a wealth that does not rot. The robe of Christ's perfect righteousness cannot be eaten by moths. Nor will the golden street of heaven ever see tarnish.

We need never fear having the true wealth Jesus gives us to be taken from us because it cannot perish. It is a wealth earned not by the sweat of exploited laborers, but through the bloody sweat of the Son of God. He perfectly obeyed the commandments of God and voluntarily suffered for us and in our place. It is a wealth which justifies us before God and allows us to live in his very presence forever. We can and must walk the talk of our faith in Christ.

John Wesley, the founder of Methodism, in one of his classic sermons on the use of money, said: "Gain all you can, save all you can, and give all you can." In the same sermon, he went on to say, "You should be continually learning, from the experience of others, or from your own experience, reading, and reflection, to do everything you have to do better today than you did yesterday. And see that you practice whatever you learn, that you may make the best of all that is in your hands."

The *Wesley Study Bible* notes that, according to Wesley, "wealth is dangerous because it can corrupt and lead to sin. Whatever our level of income, desiring more than is necessary to sustain our families and ourselves is morally destructive. Riches lure us from sharing with those in need and toward exploiting and isolating the poor for selfish financial gain. The dangers of wealth also harm the rich by leading into a self-centered lifestyle, a false sense of moral superiority, a distorted understanding of divine favor, and to the destruction and negligence of those in need."

These traits are in absolute opposition to God's character and God's expectation of his people. When blessed with more than what we need, the excess should be shared.

Look for opportunities to give the resources God has blessed you with. If God has blessed you with wealth, look for opportunities to give it away prudently. If God has blessed you with great abilities, use them for His glory.

Wise words. We must live this 24/7 faith. There is no other best option in our journey of faith from earth to heaven.

Words to Live by from the Church Fathers

CAESARIUS OF ARLES: *Riches cannot harm a good person, because he spends them kindly. Likewise they cannot help an evil person as long as he keeps them avariciously or wastes them in dissipation.*

BEDE: *Think how great is the wickedness of those who not only refuse to share their wealth with the poor and needy but who go one step further and refuses to pay their works the wages which are due them!*

CHRYSOSTOM: *What then? Has luxury been condemned? It certainly has – so why do you continue to strive for it? A man has made bread, but the excess has been trimmed away. A man has made wine, but the excess has been cut off there also. God desires that we should pray not for impure food but for souls set free from excess. For everything that God has created is good, and nothing which has been received with thanks is to be despised.*

OECUMENIUS: *James makes their possession of wealth and their stinginess a source of lamentation for those who store up their riches for burial and loss rather than give them to the needy. For the person who gives his wealth to the poor does not lose it but keep every penny. This is why the Preacher said: Cast your bread upon the waters, " that is, upon the apparent corruption and decadence of this world, and it will not be lost, but rather it will preserve us from destruction.*

CYRIL OF ALEXANDRIA: *Some people go on endless journeys for the sake of business and the profits which they can make thereby, enduring even sea travel for their sake. Some fight in order to get some advantage over others by increasing their power. Still others fatten their purses by cheating and by extortion, bringing down fire and brimstone on their heads.*

8

OTHER SNIPPETS OF HARD TRUTHS

"It is a sin when someone knows the right thing to do and doesn't do it." (James 4:16)

In this "gospel of common sense" known as the Book of James we have looked at the major themes of trials, temptations, faith and works, obedience to God's word, the tongue, prejudice, poverty and wealth.

But that is not all there is in James. There are some important snippets in James as well. A snippet is a small part or piece of something or a brief extract. Something needs to be said about these snippets – they give us a brief look on the inside of some hard truths that are also important to live out.

The snippet of wisdom from below and above. You will find this snippet in James 3:13-18. If you are genuinely filled with good and godly wisdom your conduct will show it.

A truly wise person, from God's perspective, is the person who recognizes that arrogance, jealousy and selfish ambition ultimately accomplish nothing of eternal value. Wisdom recognizes and embraces that humility is more like Christ, that humility actually achieves more beneficial results than does pride and self-promotion.

It leads to purity of life, a life untouched by the sort of immoral behavior that stains the soul. The person filled with God's wisdom hates conflict unless it is in defense of the truth. The man or woman who is always quick to engage in verbal warfare and has a combative spirit is not energized by the wisdom that comes from God. James appeals to us to turn our energy toward unity and conciliation rather than division and alienation.

There is more. When you are filled with and governed by the wisdom from above, your life will be filled with mercy and good actions. Your interaction with and evaluation of others will be peaceful and gentle. And your commitment to live in peace and to pursue peace with others will sow the seeds of justice and love by peaceful acts.

The snippet of conflict with people and God. A Canadian pastor told a true story of how a new denomination got started in that country. It all started the night that a Mr. Horner was enthusiastically preaching when his tie became wrapped around his hand. He concluded that the devil was trying to bind him in his preaching. So he tore off his tie, threw it on the ground, stomped on it, and said that ties were from the devil.

From then on he taught that Christians ought never to wear ties because they bound them in their Christian lives. Others disagreed, which led to quarrels, which led to division. Today in Canada, there is a tie-less group called the "Hornerites."

If you are as I, you may find it incredulous that such could happen. It is disconcerting that Christians would quarrel over such a trivial matter.

But I have been around church and pastoral ministry long enough to see it happen, sadly enough. I recall when I was in Bible college and traveling with a male quartet during the summer in public relations for the college. We were scheduled to sing at a church that had made quite a big deal

about how wide the tie is and what kind of watch was worn –
whether it was plain, gold, or silver. Furthermore, there was a
big deal made about the length of our 70s style trimmed
sideburns! You can probably guess what we did that night as a
group of college guys hardly in our 20s. We stopped at a
service station in town, nearby the church, to trim our
sideburns to the "right" length. And yes, that night, in order to
be able to minister effectively on behalf of the college, we
wore no ties with our suits and we made sure our watches
were not showing beyond the length of our suit coats or took
them off for the concert that night. As I look back on this, I
think – what folly! And all because a group of people in a
church took something quite trivial and made something very
spiritual out of it. I often wonder what unbelievers must think
of such things. Maybe we should ask them!

Sometimes, when serious doctrinal issues are at stake,
division among professing Christians is demanded. If we
compromise the gospel, we are no longer Christian in any
meaningful sense of the word. But, sadly, all too often our
divisions and quarrels are over petty matters, not essentials.

What is true among churches is also true in our homes.
Many Christian homes are wracked by conflict rather than
permeated with the sweet aroma of the peace of Christ.

So it was not a unique situation when James addressed
the problem of quarrels and conflicts among the believers to
whom he wrote in James 4. It applies to all of our relational
conflicts, whether in the church or at home.

The overall idea may be summed up: To resolve
conflicts, repent of your sinful selfishness and humble yourself
before God. To resolve conflicts, judge your selfish motives.

To resolve conflicts, turn away from the world, give total allegiance to God, and humbly seek His grace. To resolve conflicts, submit to God, resist the devil, and in God's presence repent of all your sins. To resolve conflicts, stop judging others and submit to God's Word.

The way to resolve conflict with others is not to win the war with others. Rather, it is to wage war against those powerful forces that are waging war in your soul! Judge your selfish motives, daily put self on the cross, and you will move in the direction of peace in your relationships.

The snippet of courageous patience. "See how the farmer waits" says James in James 5. He ploughs his field and plants his seed and then he waits for the rains. He has two grounds for patient hope - the covenant promise of God that spring times and harvests will not cease, and then, his experience over many years of the truth of that word. So, it is not irrational for the farmer to clear his land, dig the furrows and scatter the corn. The farmer has the experience of the Lord's fulfilled promises to sustain him. God has set a timetable and the farmer has learned patience for its fulfillment.

In the same way, God has a time for everything he brings into our lives. We are ignorant of his schedule but we are not unaware of his sovereignty, nor of our duty. Resentment in our lives often gets focused on why God delays or why he permits pain to hit us. He does not make us privy to his reasons for our sufferings, but he gives every one of his people grace to cope with them and he tells us "be patient." Every day we receive the providence of God.

Nothing can rob us of that. Everything comes at the right time. God's clock keeps perfect time in our lives!

It is all a matter of the inner life. "Firm up your hearts" is how Jay Adams understands the idea of courageous patience. He says, "Unless you are firm within, you will not endure; with that stability you will be able to handle whatever comes your way. Inner firmness is not hard-heartedness, indifference, or some species of stoicism. That to which James refers is true, stalwart, unflinching solidity that comes from a staunch commitment to God's promises. It is a command to become impervious to pressure; it is a call to abandon all spiritual weaknesses that cause us to fall apart when the waiting is long and the struggle is intense. According to James, outer firmness is an index to inner strength of heart." We can be firm with courageous patience.

The snippet of swearing, praying, and caring. The final subjects James talks about in 24/7 living are swearing, praying and caring – all in the closing words of James 5.

When it comes to James' mention of swearing by an oath, it seems that he is actually referring to the widespread practice of dishonesty. People simply were *not* honest. They were untrustworthy and could not be counted upon. One never knew when their word was true and so there grew up the practice of oath taking to insure honesty. In certain dealings where a person's trustworthiness was essential an oath would be taken but in all other areas his or her word meant nothing. James reminds us that just guaranteeing our word by an oath is not enough; Christians always should he honest.

There is really no reason why a Christian should ever use an oath, though our legal system requires it. In every situation our word ought to be trustworthy. We do not have to take an oath in order to guarantee the truthfulness of any statement. And we don't need to "swear on a stack of Bibles" as I have heard some people say. Even our most casual conversation ought to be characterized by utter, absolute truthfulness.

Christians, of all people, know the truth. So, there should never be any reason why anything but truth would come out of our mouth and our lives. If we tell someone that we are going to be somewhere at a designated time, then we should be there. If we give our word that we will accomplish some task, then we do well to accomplish it. If we describe something that we have seen or heard, then our testimony should be in line with the truth.

There is another thing here in James 5. James recognizes that life is made up of triumph and tragedy, of sorrow and joy. We never know what to expect. Life is totally unpredictable. Life can change so radically - in just a matter of a few seconds. We never know what is ahead. That is the way life is.

And yet James says that in every circumstance of life we are to pray. There is one constant factor in our life and that is Jesus Christ. Everything must be related to him. Our circumstances change. Our emotions change. People change. Our attitudes change. But the one thing that never changes is our Lord Jesus.

Stability in our life comes from relating everything to God. If you are suffering, James says, then pray. If you are cheerful, then give thanks, sing psalms, and sing praises to God. Relate everything to Jesus Christ because he is the one who does not change. He is the same - yesterday, today, and forever.

Finally, something is said about confessing our sins to one another and praying for one another so that we may be healed. This is something that all members of the body of Christ are to do. The church is a fellowship of *mutual* concern. So, if a brother or sister is struggling with sin in his or her life and can find no deliverance, the command is to share this area of defeat with another person who will pray for them. The result will be healing. When we confess something it means that we "say the same thing out" – to agree with what God has said about sin and to agree openly. We are not to defend sin in our life. We are not to cover it up. We are to agree openly with God about it.

We know already that practicing our faith means that we will have the fruit of good deeds in our life. Perhaps there is no stronger illustration of this than visiting the sick. When we visit the sick, as Christians we have the opportunity to identify with those in need just as Christ identified with the "least of these."

In John Wesley's Sermon 98, "On Visiting the Sick," Wesley admonishes us to visit both the good and the bad because God's grace seeks all persons. Visiting the sick becomes a means through which we partake of God's gift of healing ministry. Visiting the sick overcomes the isolation often experienced by the sick. The sick, the suffering, and the poor are brought into grace-filled relationship. Those who visit become Christ-bearers who grow in love and compassion.

We are reminded here that there are some things in our lives that we cannot cope with alone. There may even be perpetual and chronic habits that have such a grip on people's lives that there is no way to find deliverance alone. All of us need the strength of the Christian community of faith. We cannot travel alone. And if we go to another member of the body of Christ, someone who loves us and cares for us, and if we share our area of defeat with them openly, and if they pray for us, there can be healing. And the prayer of faith will save the sick.

The snippet of rescuing wanderers from the faith. Throughout this book James has revealed the truth to us. His final word in James 5:19-20 is: "My brothers and sisters, if any of you wander from the truth and someone turns back the wanderer, recognize that whoever brings a sinner back from the wrong path will save them from death and will bring about the forgiveness of many sins."

Here is a clear reminder that there is every possibility that members of the family – our brothers and sisters in Christ - will stray. We all sense that there is a tendency on the part of all of us to stray from the truth.

What happens when a member of the body strays? Does James say to criticize them, to ostracize them, to cut them off, to turn your back on them? Absolutely not! He says to turn the wanderer from the wrong path. Rescue them! Go to them in love and restore them.

Paul writes in Galatians 6: "Brothers and sisters, if a person is caught doing something wrong, you who are spiritual should restore someone like this with a spirit of gentleness." Restore them. "Carry each other's burdens and so you will fulfill the law of Christ."

I remember hearing the story of a boy who was trudging through the ghetto with a little crippled boy on his back. The boy was asked how he could carry such a heavy load. He responded, "He ain't heavy. He's my brother!"

When we see a brother or a sister who is falling it is our responsibility to go to them, to pick them up and support them, to encourage them and turn them back to the truth.

James says that the result will be that we will turn a sinner from the error of his or her way. We will save a soul from death. We, through love, will cover a multitude of sins.

Sadly enough, it has been said that Christians are the only ones who shoot and kill their wounded! This ought not to be!

What about saving a soul from death? James uses death metaphorically in this book. He is not referring primarily to physical death but rather to the death-like state that exists when people fail to respond to the truth. We have all experienced this death - the boredom, frustration, and emptiness which is the consequence of disobedience to the truth.

James says that when someone wanders away from the truth we are to go to that brother or sister and lovingly restore them. In this way we will save their soul from that death-like state of living and we will cover a multitude of sins – we will secure forgiveness for them.

Now, those two actions - salvation from death and forgiveness of sins - are the actions of God. Only God can save a soul from death. And only God can forgive sins. And yet we are given the privilege of being a co-worker with God. We can do what He is doing in the lives of people and can share with Him in the ministry of restoration. We can help bring about reconciliation. These are most awesome words!

And here James ends his letter quite abruptly. There is no benediction, no doxology, no gesture of farewell. It is as though he does not want to deflect our minds from the privilege and responsibility of living out what it means to live 24/7 in the life-giving power of Jesus Christ within us. We do this when we confess to one another, when we pray for one another and when we care for one another.

Some final words. If it seems that this book has been stomping on your toes, it is only because James stomps on all of our toes! He is not just a nice, polite man who beats around the bush in a mealy-mouthed manner. He is a doctor of the soul who speaks the truth plainly, even when it hurts. But you should prefer a doctor who speaks the truth over one who is nice but never tells you what is wrong.

If you will heed James' straightforward analysis your life and your relationships will improve dramatically! You will live the Christian life 24/7 and in the end that is what life in and through Jesus Christ is truly all about.

One more thing. Many years ago when I established my personal e-mail, I wanted a short, easy-to-remember, pithy line under my name that expresses a motto for my life. And when someone reads that far down in the e-mail below my name they will also see it. It is this: "Live . . . so as not to regret a single moment." That, my reader friend, is 24/7 living. Live with no regrets. Do no harm. Do good. And stay in love with God. That is the maxim for Christian living – every day.

SERENITY PRAYER (FOR TODAY)

God, grant me the **Serenity** (tranquility, composure and peace) to **ACCEPT** (gratefully receive) the things I cannot change (others, outcomes and old stuff),
COURAGE to change the things I can (my feelings, attitudes and behaviors/choices), and **WISDOM** (understanding) to know the difference . . .
LIVING One Day at a time . . .
ENJOYING One MOMENT at a time (mindfully observing, describing and participating) in **The Precious Present** . . .
ACCEPTING HARDSHIP as a pathway to **PEACE** . . .
TAKING, as Jesus did, this sinful (wicked, corrupt and broken) world as it **IS**, not as I would have it . . .
TRUSTING that You are making all things right as I **SURRENDER** (give in) to **YOUR** will . . . So that I am reasonably (sensibly and quite) **HAPPY** in this life and **SUPREMELY HAPPY** with You forever in the next.
AMEN. (So be it!)

> Adapted from Reinhold Niebuhr's original prayer
> by Heidi Vermeer-Quist
> *www.gardeningmylife.com*

APPENDIX

A Potpourri on the Book of James

It may well be that when you see or hear the word "potpourri" you think of a mixture of flowers, herbs, and spices that is usually kept in a jar and used for scent. And, for sure, that is an appropriate dictionary definition. However, the word potpourri has another definition. It can mean a miscellaneous collection.

So what I offer here is a sort of potpourri on the book of James – some things that are tidbits of information that put the Book of James in a nutshell. It is information that makes things easy to remember about the Book of James. So, in bullet point fashion, here is some potpourri for you.

- James, the "brother" of Jesus, is traditionally considered the author of the book of James.
- James was written perhaps somewhere around 49 A.D., by best estimates of biblical scholars.
- It is the 59th book in the Bible, as listed in the Old Testament and New Testament order of books.
- It is the 20th book in the New Testament order of books.
- It is the 15th of twenty-one Epistle Books.
- Seven books follow it in the New Testament.
- There are 5 chapters in the book, 108 verses, 2,309 words in the Authorized Version.
- Traditionally, James was the brother of Jesus who was given the title *James the Just*.
- James was one of the "pillar leaders" of the church in Jerusalem.

- James was a central figure at the Jerusalem Council in Acts 15.
- According to the Jewish historian Flavius Josephus, James suffered a martyr's violent death in A.D. 62.
- The Book of James is addressed to Hebrews outside of Palestine - "to the twelve tribes which are scattered abroad." (1:1)
- The Book of James may be one of the earliest writings in the New Testament.
- There is no mention of Gentile Christians or their relationship to Jewish Christians.
- James does not mention the issues that he discussed during the Acts 15 council at Jerusalem.
- There are more than thirty-five indirect references to the teaching of Jesus in the epistle, twenty-five of which come from the Sermon on the Mount.
- James is often cited as the "Proverbs" of the New Testament.
- In the Book of James, the word "faith" occurs 12 times, the word "works" occurs 13 times, and the word "doers" occurs 5 times (*Authorized Version*)
- James has a lot to say about faith versus works.
- Faith without works cannot be called faith at all.
- Faith without works is dead, and a dead faith is worse than no faith at all.
- Faith must work.
- Faith must produce.
- Faith must be visible.
- Faith displays itself in works.
- Faith is more than mere words.

- Faith is more than knowledge.
- Faith is demonstrated by obedience.
- Faith overtly responds to the promises of God.
- Verbal faith is not enough; and mental faith is insufficient.
- Faith must be there, but it must be more, it must inspire action.
- Faith endures trials.
- Faith obeys the word. It will not merely hear and not do.
- Faith helps control the tongue.
- Faith gives us the ability to resist the devil and humbly draw near to God.
- Faith gives us the ability to choose wisdom that is heavenly and to shun the wisdom that is earthly.
- Faith waits patiently for the coming of the Lord.

The Least Favorite Laws Of Life

Life is difficult. It will include suffering.

God loves us, but that does not entitle us to special treatment because God loves everyone else just as much.

Life does not come with any guarantees.

Our bodies can malfunction and are subject to injury and illness.

Bad things happen to good people.

There are no magic potions, no panaceas.

Not everyone we meet will like us.

The more we genuinely love and care about another human being, the more anxiety we experience concerning their well-being.

Every advantage is accompanied by a disadvantage.

The disasters that actually befall us in our life are often ones we never even considered.

Money, even lots of money, can only buy things that can be bought.

Sometimes our worst fears do come true.

Everything changes.

Just because we love someone, it does not mean that they will love us in return.

Some of our most cherished dreams may not come true, no matter how much we want them to.

The chances are very high that we never got all our important needs met in childhood. Nevertheless, we are completely responsible for who we are today.

Sometimes there are no second chances.

Despite the human relationships we have, we remain separate individuals and face life (and death) alone.

Life is not always fair, at least in the short run of one lifetime.

Evil exists.

We will never be free of problems because every solution inevitably creates a new problem.

Our defenses can keep us from experiencing love and peace.

Without our defenses we would be absolutely terrified.

Because we inevitably hurt and are hurt by one another, we need to forgive ourselves and each other endlessly.

We really are going to die.

Our time of death is unknown; it may occur today.

Our manner of death is also unknown; it may be painful.

Because life involves anxiety, pain and suffering, we desperately need each other's love and acceptance.

The Least Favorite Laws of Life apply to all of us.

> (from *Finding Serenity in the Age of Anxiety* by Robert Gerson)

PRAYER OF FRANCIS OF ASSISI

Francis (1186-1226) was born in Assisi, in the Umbrian region of Italy, to a wealthy fabric merchant and his wife. He grew up taking full advantage of his fortunate circumstances. He traveled, spent money freely, and lived a self-indulgent life. He was said to be charming, charismatic, and generous.

Even war did not tame his spirits. He went off to fight in a conflict and was taken prisoner. He spent a year in jail and then succumbed to a serious illness. His recovery was slow. Both experiences brought about a spiritual crisis. Francis gave serious thought to the way he had been living, and decided to make a pilgrimage to Rome in 1206.

A different Francis returned home. He resolved to devote his life to serving the poor and the sick. His father thought he was insane – and went so far as to disinherit him.

Francis eventually retreated to a small chapel, the Portiuncula, to devote his life to preaching and to the poor. He soon began attracting disciples, who were at first curious about the rich boy who had given everything away. Among those interested in the saint's work were several prominent citizens of Assisi. With all of those willing workers in mind, Francis founded the Franciscan order in 1209, which continues to this day. It would be dedicated to absolute poverty, humility, and the love of all created things.

This beautiful prayer, worthy to be prayed each day, is traditionally attributed to him. It remains one of my favorites.

Lord, make me an instrument of your peace;
where there is hatred, let me sow love;
where there is injury, pardon;
where there is doubt, faith;
where there is despair, hope;
where there is darkness, light;
and where there is sadness, joy.

O Divine Master,
grant that I may not so much seek
to be consoled as to console;
to be understood, as to understand;
to be loved, as to love;
for it is in giving that we receive,
it is in pardoning that we are pardoned,
and it is in dying that we are born to Eternal Life.
Amen.

PREACHING AND TEACHING NOTES
SOURCES FOR 24/7 LIVING:
HARD TRUTHS FROM JAMES

Barclay, William. *The New Daily Study Bible, The Letters of James and Peter.* Louisville: Westminster John Knox Press, 2003.

Gerson, Robert. *Finding Serenity in the Age of Anxiety.* New York, NY: Bantam Books, Macmillan Publishing, 1997.

Johnson, Earl S., Jr. *James, First and Second Peter, First, Second and Third John, Basic Bible Commentary, Volume 28.* Nashville: Abingdon Press, 1988.

Life Application Bible Commentary. *James.* Carol Stream, IL: Tyndale House, 1992.

Moo, Douglas. Tyndale New Testament Commentary. *James.* Grand Rapids: Eerdmans Publishing Co., 1985.

Motyer, J.A. *The Message of James: The Tests of Faith.* Downers Grove: InterVarsity Press, 1985.

Oden, Thomas C. and Gerald Bray, eds. *Ancient Christian Commentary on Scripture, New Testament XI, James-Jude.* Downers Grove: InterVarsity Press, 2000.

Oden, Thomas C. *John Wesley's Teachings, Volume 4: Ethics and Society.* Grand Rapids: Zondervan, 2014.

Quicknotes Simplified Bible Commentary Series. *Volume 12: Hebrews thru Revelation.* Uhrichsville, OH: Barbour Publishing, Inc., 2008.

Rienecker, Fritz. *Linguistic Key to the Greek New Testament.* Grand Rapids: Zondervan, 1980.

Shepherd's Notes. *James.* Nashville: B&H Publishing Group, 1998.

Schroedel, Jenny. *The Book of Saints: Inspirational Stories and Little-Known Facts.* New York: Fall River Press, 2007.

The Wesleyan Bible Commentary. *Volume VI, Hebrews-Revelation.* Grand Rapids: Wm. B. Eerdmans Publishing Co., 1966.

The Wesley Study Bible. *NRSV.* Nashville: Abingdon Press, 2009.

The New Interpreters Bible. *Volume XII, Hebrews-Revelation.* Nashville: Abingdon Press, 1998.

Tozer, A.W. *The Root of the Righteous.* Chicago: Moody Publishers, 1955, 1986.